I Want to Live

Writers for Humanity

inner child press international

'building bridges for cultural understanding'

CREDITS

Authors
Writers for Humanity

Editor
hülya n. yılmaz, Ph. D.

Cover Design
William S. Peters, Sr.
Inner Child Press International

General Information

I Want to Live

Writers for Humanity

1st Edition: 2021

This Publishing is protected under Copyright Law as a "Collection". All rights for all submissions are retained by the individual author and / or artist. No part of this publishing may be reproduced, transferred in any manner without the prior WRITTEN CONSENT of the "Material Owner" or its Representative, Inner Child Press. Any such violation infringes upon the Creative and Intellectual Property of the Owner pursuant to International and Federal Copyright Law. Any queries pertaining to this "Collection" should be addressed to Publisher of Record.

Publisher Information:

Inner Child Press
intouch@innerchildpress.com
www.innerchildpress.com

This Collection is protected under U.S. and International Copyright Laws

Copyright © 2021: Inner Child Press

ISBN-13: 978-1-952081-42-2 (inner child press, ltd.)

$ 19.95

Dedication

This book is dedicated to

Humanity, Peace & Poetry

The power of the pen

can effectuate change!

*Poets and Writers
sowing seeds in the
Conscious Garden of Life,
that those who have yet to come
may enjoy the Flowers.*

Table of Contents

Preface — xiii
A Few Words from the Director of Editing Services — xv
Disclaimer — xvii

The Poetry

Anthony Arnold	3
Solomon C. Jatta	4
Maid Corbic	5
Ram Krishna Singh	6
Srutakirti Tripathy	7
Ujjal Mandal	9
Tapas Dey	10
Nandita De nee Chatterjee	11
Neha Bhandarkar	13
Ashok Kumar	14
Ali Al Hazmi	15
Germina Melius	16
Bob McNeil	17
Hussein Habasch	18
Debaprasanna Biswas	20

Table of Contents ... *continued*

Mohammed Abdul Aziz Shmeis	21
Eliza Segiet	22
Sumaya Al-Hamaydeh	23
Mohammad Ikbal Harb	24
Suranjit Gain	26
Othmen Mahdi	27
Magdalena Jovanova	28
Julius Joy Oluwaseun	30
C. S. P. Shrivastava	31
Jyoti Nair	32
Alicja Maria Kuberska	33
D' Siafa Draper	35
Obinna Chilekezi	36
Akshaya Kumar Das	37
Ibrahim Honjo	38
Chinedu Jonathan Ichu	40
Thirupurasundari C. J.	41
Anjana Prasad	43
MTK	45
Robert Anthony Gibbons	46
Shareef Abdur-Rasheed	48

Table of Contents... *continued*

Eden Soriano Trinidad	50
Tono	51
Hasan Asy'ari	52
Smruti Ranjan Mohanty	53
Pepe Wibowo	55
Noreen Ann Snyder	56
Olaoye Olawale Olufemi	57
Amb Lovelyn P. Eyo	58
Aruna Bose	60
Tara Noesantara	61
Yanz Haryo Darmista	62
Padmapriya Karthik	63
Monsif Beroual	64
Alicia Minjarez Ramirez	65
Alonzo Gross	66
hülya n. yılmaz	68
William S. Peters, Sr.	71

Essays, Analyses and Stories

Mutawaf A. Shaheed	77

Table of Contents... *continued*

Shareef Abdur-Rasheed	83
Gail Weston Shazor	87
hülya n. yılmaz	91
William S. Peters, Sr.	95

Voices Behind the Wire

Introduction by William S. Peters, Sr.	*101*
Shaylor Watson	102
Ben "Solo" Martinez	104
Charles Baker	106
Ras'safidi	109
Anthony Hawk Hoskins	111
Haneef Walid	114
Antwan Carter	115
Matt Shepard	116
Rodney "Peddiewack" Glaze	117
Douglas/E'Vone Dawkins	118
Jonathon Gordon	120
Ivan Kilgore	123

Table of Contents... *continued*

Sitawa Nantambu Jamaa, James "Baridi" Williamson, Yusuf Bey IV, and Ivan Kilgore	131
Abdur Nadheerūl-Islam	141
Kevin Curley	144
Stephen Wilson	147
Lonnie B. English Bey	150
Wayland "X" Coleman	152
Donnie Phillips	154
Raymond Springs II	155
Brandon Dixon	159

Epilogue

About Inner Child Press International	165
Other Socially Important Anthologies by ICPI	169

Poets, Writers . . . know that we are the enchanting magicians that nourish the seeds of dreams and thoughts . . . it is our words that entice the hearts and minds of others to believe there is something grand about the possibilities that life has to offer and our words tease it forth into action . . . for you are the Poet, the Writer to whom the Gift of Words has been entrusted . . .

~ wsp

Preface

As the publisher and as a writer/poet as well, I think that this particular project is one of the most important efforts we, at Inner Child Press International, have embarked upon when it comes to the subject of 'Human Bias'. As a 'Black Man', it is hard for me to consider the state of things – past, present and future – outside the 'subjective' position I occupy. I realized a long time ago that there is another side of the coin of perspective that should be examined and spoken on through the 'objective' voice of writers and poets from all over the world . . . hence, *I Want To Live*.

In the end, my only hope is that more minds and hearts will allow themselves to openly embrace without prejudice the possibilities of the human genome and what can become, when we decide that we are all in this together. I, being a man of color, am not unlike you . . . I want to live.

Thank you
Bless Up

William S. Peters, Sr.

Poet, Writer, Activist, Publisher
Inner Child Press International

'building bridges of cultural understanding'

In the darkness of my life
I heard the music
I danced...
and the Light appeared
and I dance

Janet P. Caldwell

A Few Words from the ...
Director of Editing Services

Inner Child Press International ended the year of 2020 with *Poetry ~ The Best of 2020* and is welcoming 2021 with *I Want to Live.* In the likes of the previously published anthologies, including *Corona . . . Social Distancing, World Healing World Peace 2020, The Heart of a Poet, W. A. R. ~ We Are Revolution* and the one mentioned first, also this literary collection offers a multitude of creative voices worldwide.

There is one dominant trait in all of the volumes mentioned above: the vast richness of resourceful expressions. Languages represented vary between Hindi, Arabic, Polish, Italian, Nepali, Czech, Spanish, Russian, German, Indonesian, Danish, Indonesian, Filipino, Hungarian, Azerbaijani and Urdu. Also in this offering, some poems are offered to you, dear reader, in native tongues, which provides all of us with an intimate insight into the process of creative writing when absolute authenticity is concerned. The English versions then help us appreciate the dynamics between content, context and the linguistic disposition.

In specific reference to the discipline of editing, my perception also this time around will echo my words with which you might already be familiar from our previous publications. The protocol in employing editorial steps within the context of a globally-oriented book does, after all, not differ markedly with specific regard to ICPI's primary concern: to preserve the original entries in order to maintain the integrity of each literary contribution. Adopting this principle becomes particularly vital in the case of the genre of poetry. Editing does not and should not equate sacrificing the authenticity of the writer. Accordingly, we have applied minimal surface editing throughout this offering. While these points cannot be stressed strongly enough, some specifics regarding our editorial work for our anthologies are in order.

Whenever a large body of work of any literary genre is compiled, form-specific but also presentational challenges arise, even then when all writings originate from a single language. The compilation process presents a proportionately greater challenge as more language sources emerge. Texts of non-native English speakers or their own translations of those texts into English comprise contextual nonconformities. This fact is nothing out of the ordinary. Some scholars of the field may argue that all such submissions should be edited scrupulously before they are presented to the public. My professional stance differs from those colleagues based on one critical principle: editing is not the exact science one would expect. When an editor forces the rules of English upon a creative work that might not have its origin in English, the authors' authentic self-representation can easily be subjected to a misrepresentation. Writings with a dialectal, colloquial or eclectic style are exposed to the same risk when the scrutiny of editing is concerned. Too often, the resulting loss of the authorial voice can be profound and deprive the reader of the genuine aspects of a writer's thoughts, feelings and innate flavor. At Inner Child Press International, we strive to maintain the integrity of each literary gift by preserving the seemingly-awkward expressions of those whose native language is not of our own.

Our invitation to you, dear reader, remains the same as with our past anthologies: to take time to indulge each contributor for her / his own creativity and aspirations to convey her / his uniqueness.

hülya n. yılmaz, Ph.D.

Professor Emerita, The Pennsylvania State University
Director of Editing Services, Inner Child Press International

Disclaimer

In our attempts to maintain the integrity of the contributors' voices in the publication before you, *I Want to Live*, we have elected to do minimal surface editing. We felt that preserving the original entries was critically important for you, the reader, to enjoy the authenticity of each literary giving.

All poetry submissions have been preserved in their original versions, while only minor adjustments have been employed on the section of short prose. You may encounter some challenges in achieving total clarity of the messages shared through poems, but I indulge you to let go of your critical thinking and embrace the spirit through words offered for the poetic art.

From the desk of . . .
hülya n. yılmaz, Ph.D.
Director of Editing Services

Inner Child Press International
'building bridges of cultural understanding'

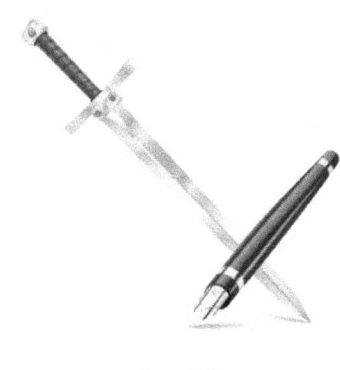

WHAT WOULD **LIFE** BE WITHOUT A LITTLE **POETRY?**

Poetry

Writers for Humanity

Red Summer
Anthony Arnold

A time when the streets ran red
With the blood of African Americans
With the intent
Of wiping them from the face of the earth

Red summer

Chicago

Black men returning from WW1
Worldly men, no longer just second class
Exceptions were taken
38 were killed

Washington D.C

The Navy, Army, and Marine Corp responded
An alleged sexual assault
A white woman was supposedly jostled
Mob mentality ruled
15-40 died. 140 injured

Philadelphia

Multiple riots in the city
Keyed by the great migration from the south
Again mob mentality was the face of the day
Yet few died.

I could continue
But why should I
The deaths were in the hundreds
An attack on the black community.

Just like Black Wall Street, Rosewood, Philadelphia 1983

'kingpen'

Save Us the Lie
Solomon C. Jatta

Save us the lie
"All men are born equal",
When BLACKS are all that cheaply die.
Why the different qual?

In Africa, peaceful a sleep, we slept,
None begged for your lands then failing.
You came forcing us away, we reluctantly left
Crying, wailing yet you kept sailing.

Slavery killed the African in me,
Beaten to put on the garments of a strange culture.
Now that America/Europe is born and grew up in me
Why seek to remove me from its future?

Don't dare tell me to go home!
When here is all I know as my Rome.

We All Have Equal Rights
Maid Corbic

People are born to love each other
And they don't divide based on skin color
Because we all have equal rights to live
And no one can take that away from us

Only immoral and dishonest people can
What their blood is blue, cold
To the touch when it flows from the body
Which repels everyone around;

And forces that are used just like that
They can be prevented by talking honestly
And not the blows we see often
For injustice hurts everyone;

And the punishment will come to every inhabitant of God
What he thinks of others is ugly and discriminating
He publicly lynches and spits on other cultures
Raising himself from the ashes of that
What roots he has long since let go!

The Ghetto
Ram Krishna Singh

I feel the yellow leaves with the day's silence in their stare

The ghetto uncovers what they try to conceal—

Feeling stuck, a little 'off', or foggy

In the sameness of everyday celebrating

No sex, no travel, no drinks, no books but black smoke

Dust and emptiness of years they're unsure about

Here each one sounds too profound, perching for new life

Between the parentheses ending up

A kite snapped and strayed into a bush.

The Coronation of a Phoenix
Srutakirti Tripathy

as she took birth
Granny shouted loudly
"Ah! she is dark
who will marry her?"
mother's heart shattered in pain
she turned her face aside
wiping eyes in silence!

dark coloured girls are never unfortunate;
can their good deeds,
hide behind their colours?
certainly
there is the radiant colour of their hearts
blood speaks . . .
no one needs rays of light
until it is dark all over
difficult may be
to read the ghastly masks
that the bright and fair face covers?

a compassionate heart wins the race
victory needs no fear
there is always the Sun
rising in the horizon
for those who work
love has no parameter of tears
dust off the cobwebs
colour discrimination is the slogan of the cowards
fear has no sting

in the depth of darkness
celebrate your dawn
precious diamonds are
buried deep under your stigma
rise up and change the enigma

for the coronation is in full swing
the Phoenix is flying high above the sky
beyond the so-called hash tags of your creation
for she is so divine . . .

A Dark Girl, the Innocent Flower!
Ujjal Mandal

An innocent flower would wake up
in her mother's lap everyday
with all sweetness.
She wanted to live but
the blood of violence began to flow
In the red sun's veins.
He decided to fade the nectar of that
sweet flower.
The sun threw the fireball over her soft
petals and beauty left her alone
in the realm of persecution
where peace cannot make a home.
When the wind came holding a sharp
weapon, the oppressed flower fell off.
Oh, she wanted to live as an innocent
and sweet flower.
Ah, my shattered heart aches!

A Voice, up in Arms
Tapas Dey

Since birth, a shroud of darksome cloud
Is over our heads.
Hopes and desires, as though, getting blurred,
Beyond the reach of fundamental touch,
All the sights and senses are shaded everywhere.

Before getting our foliated trees matured,
All leaves begin to die off.
Very common is getting despised
And going to the walls is very common.

Since childhood we are also taught,
Be the eye-shore of the racial superiority
Be injured out
Be injured in
And be on the wane.

Down the head of a blackamoor, suffocated
Under the dominant status,
And pasted on the luxurious road under the sun.

Up in arms, a little swarthy boy,
Screams in rage, "Noooooo,
This is below the belt,
Ours also are the sun and the moon,
The birth under the same canopy,
Then, why can't you, the salt of the earth,
Care for the smile of the moke kids?"

Oxygen
Nandita De nee Chatterjee

The wind whipped up over the seas
Zephyrus, the gentle God of the Wind
started his daily sojourn
through the world.
The invisible life force marked his way under the gold and silver rays
Dawn passed on to dusk
The world heaved a sigh
Gentle night arrived with its healing touch
Spreading out in every direction
it touched all living beings
old or young, bird, beast or human.
A celestial force, the ultimate power
touching all alike.
It stopped not to see the fair maiden
Blowing universally for all
Air! Which never retreats or halts
Oxygen! That which gives us life
Free and fair for all.

The Sun, the ultimate source of energy
never plays hide and seek
In clockwork precision the solar force distributes its wealth.
Equally its largesse arrives
in benevolence as in wrath.
Black, white or brown
its share never changes.
Neither the rich nor the powerful can claim it.

The Earth stands firm
never yielding ground.
Home for all, every sentient sacred
animate, inanimate – everything has a place.

The Sky, as far away and infinite to all.
Weather, never did anyone any special favours.
Blowing hot or cold, it soothes or lashes all alike.

Water! Our sustenance!
Free and fair
As all in nature.

And as the Deities deemed
Whatever be their names
However we hail them
No human being has been made special
No person given privileges
No extras for white skin or blue eyes
No discounts for being oriental or occidental
Western or Eastern.

The Wind blows from North to south
In equanimity and grace.
South, East or West
their power benign or cataclysmic
Equally affecting all.

Where the Universe never discriminates
Where the Elements exist for all
Where Man and Woman were made twice blessed
Who dares brave the wrath of the World?
Who is he to say,
I matter. You don't.
Who is he to demarcate the world?

A species dependent on the grace of the elements
calling for reprisal.
When the winds howl in fury
When the sea rises
When the earth shakes in its core
When lightning strikes from the sky
Who will it choose to spare?
Who will it choose to spare?

Black Is Blissful
Neha Bhandarkar

Though the world is not enough as it is . . .

We all live with the same colour of our blood
With the colour of our skin dark or light
Even with the colourless tears that roll down our eyes
. . . As it is!

In these days of pandemic
Entire world is observing social distancing
But we were distanced for many centuries

The Sun was shrewd & scorching to us
Due to disparity of civil rights
People shot us with their bitter words

People saw us with their bitter eyes
Sometimes we drenched in the soulful cries
Sometimes we sobbed in the rhythm of inequality & blights
The terror and fear gave our children many a sleepless night

Eradicate the tradition
Of assault upon black women
Build the bridge of courage
Unveil the mask of pretention

Let the new era of humanity be born
Let another world of peace arise
Let the world bow and realize
. . . Colorism is repulsive, painful
And sinful
But . . .
'Black is Beautiful'
'Black is Graceful'
'Black is Blissful'

A Hidden Corner of the Universe
Ashok Kumar

Let's know perfectly the narrower world of egotism

I'm the priest of poetry believe in oneness

I celebrate unity, sing melodious songs of brotherhood

Let me breathe the fragrance of love

I'm mad for universality

The divine mystery helps us to taste nectar of immortality

I'm from many nations, salute to all passion

Believe in Nature beautiful almighty creation

In the Prairies of Life
Ali Al Hazmi

Though two faces in the mirror,
A single person we are;
When you are upset, I feel it, at once.
In my veins, your hot blood flows;
You, too, feel agonized
When it is painful with me.

Some people spy on us,
Upset to see us in delight.
Displeased to see our lips smiling,
They keep throwing thorns on our way;
Yet, we will go on together
Forever.

In all conditions,
We will never be distracted by those who unleash their monsters
Into the prairies of life;
Those who have never been true humans.
Though hundreds of years passed,
Their tyrant souls were not softened.
Though the world has tasted intimacy and love
For a long time,
Those monsters still live in everlasting blindness.

You are me;
My real brother.
How gorgeous you are!
How gorgeous I become
To have you.

The Relics
Germina Melius

I heard the black woman cry, I came out to see,
a black man strangled by the relics of slavery,
a horror haunting our minds.
The black woman is mourning for her son, her people reciprocate.
Why Lord?
Who was born in the garden of ignorance, watered by hate stones?
Our oppressors – the racist ones, convey their sentiment.
They have borrowed death's hands to inflict painful scars and fill graves.
Have you ever received an epidermal license, where a price is paid?
No, I have never completed the application form for a license of colour or pain.
Walking down streets of paranoia, we drink prayerful waters
in a glass of peace and longevity, hoping for a peaceful day.
If our coffee skins were transparent like water, freely roaming the earth,
the cries of black people would cease.
I say no to the oppressors with brains of bones,
who trouble the conscience of black people like thorns, taking lives,
denying jobs, our bellies hurting, breaking bones and self-esteem.
Mental stress in augmentation, our souls need rest.
Emancipation says we belong.
Help peace, equality and justice to thrive, wash the brains of ignorance,
bind the arms of racism.

Text to Resurrect Revolution
Bob McNeil

Countee Cullen
And I are of this consensus:
Prejudice drafts psychopaths.
Their warpaths
Transfix our people to many a crucifix.
There resides the reason why
My protest must never relax
From typing its attacks.

Addressed to your psyche,
My compositions are microphones for
Emmett Till, Michael Griffith,
Yusef Hawkins, Amadou Diallo,
Sean Bell, Ramarley Graham,
Trayvon Martin, Darius Simmons,
Jordan Davis, Renisha McBride,
Eric Garner, et cetera,
Et cetera, et cetera.

Addressed to your psyche,
You can hear the murdered entreat:
"Don't allow another name to join
A homicide report sheet.
Don't allow another name to join
A homicide report sheet."

Addressed to your psyche,
The compositions
I've written are parts of a bulletin,
The passages transmit
To our terra firma's retina.

Addressed to your psyche,
My protest wants life
To evict the combustive
And discriminative.
If armed with you,
Lawfulness will live.

"I Cannot Breathe"
For George Floyd
Hussein Habasch

My hands cannot breathe
Because you handcuff them.
My feet cannot breathe
Because you put them in chains.
My heart cannot breathe
Because you withhold love from it.
My lungs cannot breathe
Because you block the air from them.
My tongue cannot breathe
Because you cut it.
My mouth cannot breathe
Because you cover it.
My neck and throat cannot breathe
Oh, remove your dirty knee from them.
I cannot breathe
I choke
I'm dying . . .!

You stole my dream
I cannot breathe.
You stole my thoughts
I cannot breathe.
You stole my land
I cannot breathe.
You stole my house
I cannot breathe.
You stole my fields, my trees, and my fruits
I cannot breathe.
You stole my homeland
I cannot breathe.
You stole my sky, my sun, my stars and my moon
I cannot breathe.

I Want to Live

You mock my skin tone
I cannot breathe.
You mock my language
I cannot breathe.
You mock my identity

I cannot breathe.
You mock my sorrow
I cannot breathe.
You mock my pain
I cannot breathe.
You mock my joy
I cannot breathe.
You mock my happiness
I cannot breathe.
You mock my smile
I cannot breathe.
You mock my depression
I cannot breathe.

You strangled, killed, imprisoned, stole, mocked . . .
But never forget: FREEDOM is coming.

Survivability
Dr. Debaprasanna Biswas

Weak mother can't rise at dawn as before
Wants her tiny girl stay up to sun rise within her lap
Mature junior wants to move faster at dawn to restaurant buckets
After then for half cup milk to a tea stall nearby for her weak mother.
There she is to wait for half an hour or more.
Mother couldn't resist her kid
Father, gatekeeper at high age got married with a lame one
Passed away by racial attack on duty before his kid
Single mother became lame once more
Helpless widow took shelter under the god own shed
Getting easy mother started cleaning job
Send daughter to evening class of an NGO
Sweet girl attracts teachers by her tenacity
Time passes by
Grown lady started thinking for street child
Symbolized her hand of the poor
Motivation against racial discrimination
Raised the slogans of right to survive.

I Want to Live
Mohammed Abdul Aziz Shmeis

Let me ask myself
What are nationalist crimes?
If I were to be
Wet with tears
What a story
The wondrous torment of my color
I collect memories of a cold
Despite the hunger
What was supported by reality
From evil as we love
And good for what we hate
From a dislocated stump
Let me just ask
Twigs of branches
Why is the hiding place
Under the stumps
It turns off and spreads
The silence of the udders
And me and he and the doors
Severed arm
I want to live
Without fear and torment
The city is simulated
Years back
Do not drink
A toast for the coming days
And do not call me
Walk over candles
I touched the bottom go with covers and shields

Hues
Eliza Segiet

This is not a color game
Everyone knows that
Green means the road is free,
Yellow is caution, something's approaching,
Red — stop.

Other hues
Don't warn, don't inform,
They really bother some
– Black to them is more than just murk.
It can't be hidden under any coat.

At times it is a curse of their existence,
Nevertheless they try showing,
Telling:
We're the same as others.
The color of our skin
Can't be a call
To kill and to destroy a human.

It's not a color game,
It's life
– The school of tolerance

Translated by Ula de B.

The Optimistic Boy
Dr. Sumaya Al-Hamaydeh

Singular by his blackness
It is as if Night has come . . .
Smiling
As if the sky rose
Has been crowned
Nicely Install silver . . .
Footsteps
Spontaneously
So we're optimistic
The moon has arrived
Like dew . . .
And it sits on the range
Playing with rain clouds
He steals from the echo poems . . .
He addresses the wishes of those who have left
In the meteorite blades . . .
Until he found his wish
He cried, blaming fate
A dream that seemed to be an illusion passed . . .
What if the beloved is colored?
It hurts if I were black lips.

I Want to Live
Mohammad Ikbal Harb

أريد أن أعيش
أريد أن أعيش خوف الفناء
أن ابتسم لزهر الاقحوان
أن أشعر بأنني إنسان
لكن النور خافت في القعر، ها هنا
حيث أنا
الهواء بارد شحيح
سرقته رطوبة الجدران
عفن الوجود طغى على الوجدان
في مزرعة روّادها بشر
يقودهم سوط طاغية جبان
هل قلت، أريد أن أعيش؟
إنها سكرة الموت... وهذا اسمه هذيان
هذيان عمره سبعون حولًا
في جيفة كان اسمها إنسان
لو كان هناك بعد الموت بعث
قد أعيش لكن ليس كإنسان
فالعبودية تتحد مع الجبان

محمد إقبال حرب

I Want to Live
Mohammad Ikbal Harb

I want to live the fear of annihilation
To smile for the chrysanthemum blossom
To feel that I am a human being
But the light is dimmed at the bottom, here
    where I am
The air is cold and scarce
It stole the moisture of the walls
The decay of existence overwhelmed the conscience
On a farm with human pioneers
They are led by the whip of a cowardly tyrant
Did I say, I want to live?
It is drunkenness . . . This is called delirium
A seventy-year-old delirium
In a carcass that was labeled human
If there was after death, he would be resurrected
I may live but not as a human being
For Slavery unites with the coward

A Black Man
Suranjit Gain

A black man lives in a town;
He has a great sorrow for own.
Men hate him all time;
God is attracted by his hymn.
Tears fall down from his eyes;
A divine being advise,
Don't cry o man don't cry!
Try to show personality try.
He says, I am black it's not my vice;
My mind is sacred and nice.
He decides to do a noble deed;
For the world which is need.
He writes a book named Humanity;
The treatise obtains very publicity.
All men are equal and god's creation;
The book's summary love and compassion.
Now he is a respected personality;
All over the world his popularity.

The Black Heart Is White
Othmen Mahdi

Painter if mixed all colors He finds the color black
A sailor who descends deep into the oceans finds darkness . . . the color black
When it bleeds, it dries up and turns black
The fire that is life gives birth to manure black
War is black, but war is giving us a great people
Death is black
The ball is black
Hatred is black
The black man loves all colors and he loves white
A black heart is white as is love, hope and honesty
That is why he loves all humanity and hates death, hatred and hatred

Душа
Магдалена Јованова

Има ли душата боја, или избор да го бира своето тело ?
Може ли да бира каде ќе се роди, во град или село?
Каде ќе заврши нејзиното добро намерно дело?
Може ли да бира во што ќе се облече, во патрали или одело?
Што сака душата црно, жолто или бело?
На овие прашања одговара секој потврдно или спротивно,
но зошто да не му докажеме на светот,
дека единствен е летот на душата,
и таа неможе да бира никаква сила,
освен онаа добронамерната на сите што ни е мила.
Да погледне лево или десно во секој агол ќе и биде тесно,
затоа не треба да бира боја само треба да ја одбере секој,
дружбата како опција своја.
Нашата безбојна душа, од претходните векови и сега,
иста е, не исчезнала, само со заблуда се опседнала, глава наведнала.
Исправи се душо и погледни околу себе, се е овде вредно како тебе и мене,
затоа подај му рака на секој што тоа од тебе го сака,
нема човекот да осети никаква мака ако до себе негува и љуби,
се што природата несака да изгуби.
Еднаквоста да владее за да не се прашуваме, нашата слобода каде е.
Никој со никој да не си замерува, за да се живее, секој треба во себе да верува.

Soul
Magdalena Jovanova

Does the soul have a colour or a choice to choose its body?
Does the soul can choose where it can be born, in a town or a village?
Does the soul can choose where it will end its act of kindness?
Can it choose how to be dressed, in wonderful suit or ripped clothes?
What the soul wants, black, yellow, or white?
To all these questions, some will agree, and some will disagree,
but why we do not prove it to the world,
that the only way is the soul liberation,
and it cannot choose any force,
except the kind one that we all desire.
To look left or right,
each corner it will find it tight.
The only option is caring,
and not the colour to define.
Our colourless soul, from centuries ago . . .
it is still the same, it has not disappeared,
it has just obsessed itself with delusion and heavy heart.
Rise up soul and look around you,
everything is precious like you and me.
So, give a hand to anyone that needs a hand,
and a man will not suffer, if gives love and cares.
Equality should win, and that is where our freedom begins.
To live a fulfilled life, everyone should be good to one another,
and must have a faith within.

A Piece of My Mind!
Julius Joy Oluwaseun

Just to give you a piece of my mind
But you left abruptly
Shutting the gates behind
I haven't said one-third of it all!
Don't mess with a royal priesthood
Or the guards take you down.

I should have ended it with hot-coal words
You proved smarter
Taking the first leave
Displayed how discourteous you've grown.

I stood up to your insolence
All you wanted was kill indolence
An offer of rational assistance
First impression lashing out violence.

"Listen to me boy" anthemed your momma
Daily, fell on invisible ears
"Courtesy takes you places"
Bruised her lips for being over said!

All you had a sense of-
Was to languish in your youth
Now in the quarter past three of your existence
You want to erase all wrongs!

Can a spoilt cracked egg be made a new?

I'll just mettle as a sage
And watch the end scene from a stone's throw.

Racial Equality
C. S. P. Shrivastava

Splashes 'n streaks
On the streets
Vouch for no colour
Other than the red!
Racism an incendiary issue
It remained –

Proponents plead holding
Racial differentiation
Cultural and gender apartness –
As a God given doctrine
Paradoxically forgetting
Obvious unity of Human race
(As founded by Adam n Eve)

Race conceived as a Social-construct
Even in the post Racial Society Racism does exist
When the pre-conceived notion Of
Racial hierarchy breathes its last n
The Scientists 'n Genetics
Amply prove – Humanity as more alike
(than unlike)!!

Let's turn a new leaf then
Fostering empathy 'gainst
Conscious or unconscious burn
With diversity n inclusiveness -
Let's kindle Hope n Awareness
More 'n more . . .

Beyond the mere
Int' l Day for the Elimination
Of R D (Racial Discrimination)
Unto the Core of
All Human Beings.

The Black Ivory – A Resurrection
Jyoti Nair

Our derma is black, we are proud of our charcoal-bedaubed narratives. Though, we are flogged and flayed, you can only have peels of our abrased skin.

The tenacious luminescence that our bones are borne with, will ceaselessly prod your conscience.

When Martin Luther King Jr, weaved his emancipated visions through the soul-jabbing dream speech,

That wasn't an obscure chimera, to be belittled.

Dream speech is an agglomeration of strangulated wails, through which ruptured veins of injustice, plastered themselves with obsidian primer.

Since eons you have been trying to bludgeon our rainbows, lambasting that our palettes be filled with graphite timidness.

That we need to asphyxiate under your barbaric knees,
And let your contaminated minds hold the reins, while we gallop as your steeds.

All through this poem, I have used the word – You.
You is in reference to those Machiavellian mindsets – (Institutions, Tenets, Dictums, Individuals, and all those that constitute that avaricious array),
Who have been constricting every throat that demonstrates the incendiary valour,
Who have been fist-throttling every gallant deed, reinforcing with all its mettle.
That equality is not a phantasmagorical allegory. That equality is that righteous acorn,
that we ought to relentlessly sow, into every oak, and steer every decision-oar with its resilience.
For the nations and outlooks that we aim to build, can't be vanquished anymore beneath trampling tyranny.

A Story About Difficult Love
Alicja Maria Kuberska

We create parallel worlds,
fence them off
and put up invisible walls.

We set patterns
of beauty, success and happiness
and we build hierarchies.
Later we climb up this wall
to look down on the others.
It's easy to feel self-esteem
– there is always somebody
worse than we are.

It is not difficult to sort people.
The dividing line can be different:
The black – the white
The fat – the slim
The ugly – the pretty
The poor – the rich

We have little tolerance.
Even on the paintings of Jesus Christ,
he is a slender young man
with blond hair and blue eyes.
It is hard to imagine him
as a dark-skinned Semite
with a humped nose.

Recently, an odd Jew
has moved to our neighborhood.
He wanders around
and wants to save the world.
People mock him and say he is crazy.
Someone spray-painted the star of David
on the door of his house,
broke his windows with stones.

Writers for Humanity

He was seen a few days ago
when he was talking to a black beggar.
He hugged and comforted her,
wiped tears from her cheeks.
They found the gate to their worlds
and they went over the walls

The Blood Diamond
D' Siafa Draper

For this diamond
They killed my father
For this diamond
They amputated my mother
For this diamond
They made me child soldier
For this diamond
They made me kill at random
For this diamond
They left me abandoned

For this diamond
Yea . . ., for this diamond

I suffered starvation
For this diamond
I had no salvation
For this diamond
I had no pardon
For this diamond
I carry scary scars
For this diamond
I'd wished my flute wore a parachute
For this diamond
My dreams were stained
For this diamond
My name was shamed
For this diamond
I strived to survive
Have I seen this diamond?
Have I touched this diamond?
O that they were blinded by demons
For which they knew no human
For this diamond
Freetown became a horror town
For this diamond
. . . I'm still in search of me.

We Are All Brown, Colourful
Obinna Chilekezi

You are not my colour
I am not your colour
And we are colourful,
See you and I in love
Seeing just the brown in-between,
As we cannot separate white and black
As in our blood

We are just beautiful
You and I
As we are all just brown
Not colour-blind, but colour-beautiful
When we love one another the more.

I Want to Live . . .
Akshaya Kumar Das

Love all be it black or white,
Same blood flows in each one of us,
The colour is blood is unique,
Does not differentiate between black & white,

I want to live a colourless life,
Live above the narrow mindedness,
Live a healthy life of purpose,
Serve the poverty-stricken people of the universe,

All men & women are equal,
By nature & character they are mortal,
Live above the mundanely possessions,
Serve the humanity at large with integrity & passion,

Remove the ugly differences between man & man,
Live above the barriers of caste, creed, colour, race & religion,
Make love not war shall be the goal of life,
Peace & happiness shall reign sans any strife.

To Live in Harmony
Ibrahim Honjo

Discrimination is a disease
A severe disease of this civilization
Why when we all originated on the same planet
All of us woven of bones of blood and flesh
All in their skins
Originated in different parts of the world

Your skin is white
Our skin is black

Originated in Africa
We live all over this planet
Torn from our homeland
You needed slaves
You needed us to have someone to trample on
Until when, white brothers
Until when

Our skin is black
We are people like you
We are all earthlings
We pray to the same God
Born each in his own skin

We want to live with everyone in harmony and peace
Have the same rights as you
Our blood is red; as is yours
Our desires are progress, happiness, peace

Discrimination is a disease
Heavy as an occupier's boot
A noose wrapped in cellophane of his rules

Our hearts beat life just like yours
Our eyes see far and high
You stifle our voice, our gaze, our rights

I Want to Live

This is our common planet
Not just yours
Not just ours

We did not choose skin color or place of birth
Our freedoms and peace taken for centuries
You do not allow us to put you in our hearts
You do not allow us to clothe you with our souls
Not even to love you as our neighbor

What God are you praying to?
What bible are you reading?

Our skin is black
Your skin is white

There is whiteness in our blackness
As there is blackness in your whiteness

You do not know or do not want to know
This thread binds us
This is where the secret fraternity rests

Yours and our homeland is planet Earth
We are all earthly
Everyone in his or her own skin

We are still alive
We want to live
In harmony, in peace, in tolerance, in equality

Discrimination is a serious disease
Yet the only cure is love

I Want to Live . . .
Chinedu Jonathan Ichu

we had done no wrong,
never orchestrated an iota of war-mongering
but like a lamb to the slaughter
we were led away unjustly
who are we to mislead anyone
we are livid nocturnal creatures,
who only settle for tainted starch
garnished inside follicles of bloated crumbs
they promised us mass burial
in a rich man's genitalia, if we sold our nativity
sugarcoated cyanide cascade down frozen lips
our beloved flag floats half-mast atop liquor
seeping out the orifice of punctuated lungs
who else has believed our epistle?
how formidable are the hurriedly dug trenches
that will stomach our despised voice
I want to live . . .
for these shackles can never mute our spirit
like ravaging pellets from the barrel of costly hate
shattering the harvest in an unwanted fetus
Heaven has begun to mourn and dry up
will all our hard work be for nothing?
in our vision, we see goblets of vast wasteland stagger
they boast and threaten to sacrifice our offspring
we envisaged our troubles were a punishment from God,
now we have been profited double edged swords . . .

Adore the Spectrum
Thirupurasundari C. J.

Mutilate racial segregation,
Pinning new hopes for future generation,
Throbbing history is not their desire,
Cynical towards a group?
Skin tone should never be a symbol,
It isn't a benchmark for any standpoint.

White supremacy and oppressed souls?
Slavery, discrimination, prejudice,
Racism and mass decimation,
Rage, guilt, abuse and grief,
Fight for power and clout?
Pull off conflict,
Pride and arrogance do nothing,
Break these clichés,
Illegitimate tyranny be uprooted!

Let optimism be our cherishing drink,
No songs of turmoil and injustice,
Woe! Riots breed perturbed minds,
None deserves such predicaments,
The rhythm of revelation shine,
Upliftment and freedom resonate,
Smarter are the youthful minds,
Arbitrate better changes and healing,
As generations pass, this topic of chagrin,
Be not discussed upon,
Revolutionary changes may seem hard and messy,
Ah! Their fruits are amazing,
Let future glorify this change,
Change for the betterment.

After all matter of pigmentation,
Oh! Naughty are the genes,
At the end all are Homo sapiens,

Celebrate this human spirit,
Never underrate anyone's ability,
Intelligence, priceless possession,
Alas! It erupts social bias?

Not to use as a gadget for oppression,
Never gauge one's intelligence,
They teach us no life lessons,
Anyone can spout nonsense any time!

Share the happiness,
Experience love,
Comprehend other's aches,
Not good to judge,
Connect naturally,
Mobilize peace,
Let love freely flow,
Spread love,
Let it ameliorate hope, faith, determination and progression.

Each one is entitled to be independent,
All are worthy enough to prosper,
Everyone deserves to be happy.

Live and let others live!
God's children are we.

'Dazzle'

A False Perception
Anjana Prasad

We all are human beings
born from a mother's womb
black, brown or white doesn't matter.
In the pandemonium of life
from dawn to dusk struggling
for subsistence
dripping sweat to survive.
For each one of us
the glory of the sun fades at dawn
every second we breathe the same air
we not different in the Lord's eyes.
Less melanin or more, does it matter?
For each one of us
red runs in our veins.
Nature never discriminates
it looks upon us the same
in bounty and blessings
in disorder and despair.
Who are we to create
the stigma of racism,
the stigma of rejection,
the stigma of shame?
What if you don't like me?
What if you hate me?
What if you judge me?
We all are travelers here
life is quite explicit
we can't choose
even if we have a choice
black-skinned or white
both kneel down afore the altar
for blessings from the same God.
Our colours are a mark from him
that can't be erased

it is a part of us,
for without black, there is no white.
Let's be brother and sisters.
Let the brotherhood prevail
for peace to sustain.

I Want to Live
MTK

blood coverings
fades of murder
black men

women and children
are witnesses
since

people of color
of other
of murder

people with
religion
with
derision

brutal color
killed,
stone

covers
in their
own blood

the black bottom
Robert Anthony Gibbons

I grew up there
in the black and red
clay road of Georgia

grandma grew me
off peaches and pears
grandma grew me

from the pig slop
called chitterlings
and she sat

on her porch
and she sat
in her hurt

it was not that
black ugly dream
but a means

to survive she
called the rainbow tide
it meant you wanted

something haunted
by the blues or
the gospel of the wind

the cornfield, not the
cotton, nor the rotten
tobacco, but we had

a mother of the blues
be it in the church
or the juke joint

I Want to Live

each sound the same
each holy ghost
has a name

came from the hurt
like the dirt.

raised . . .
Shareef Abdur-Rasheed

to give praise on Sundays
as the sunrays penetrate
through the stained glass
splashing on and past the pews
as the parishioners pray in
full view
immersed in a curious world
exclusive of those who don't
look, talk and act like you
a little bubble designed to
keep out trouble
but steeped in sin their lives
kith 'n' kin, husbands, wives
insulated from folk deemed
hated, isolated away from
people of color, that other
from whom they remain
segregated
taught bout dem 'n' those
folk ain't da same as our
folk
and they grow up confined to
this mental yoke
closed mind, blind eyez
the whole wide world has been
shrunk down to a little corner
called white folks' town, and
we don't want ya'll hanging round
and dem grow up
and become your cops, judges,
doctors, nurses, lawyers, mayors,
prison jailers and jurors given the
job to sit judgement on those same
folk who their forefathers spoke
with all the distain they invoked

I Want to Live

all the hateful jokes things they
say, day after day . . .,
poised to hand down a verdict
to put your brown 'n' black ass away
or just shot you down acting as judge 'n'
jury in yours and my town without a worry
about any sentence handed down
and who da F%^# cares
that da system call dem
jury of your peers
that without blinking will
put you away for years
or let a killer walk who walked
to stalk and kill an innocent 17 year
old boy at will, enjoying the laws that
gave him the privilege to do
it to mine 'n' yours
like it's a game playing with
toys that got souls, names
lives, sons, daughters, husbands
wives
but never does it connect
in their feeble mind speck
that the same folk of whom their
peeps spoke are human beings
who deserve the same things
beginning with . . .
respect

Food4thought = education

I Want to Live
Eden Soriano Trinidad

I want to live although the world is full of anguish
and disarray enigmatic hues.
White is a color, and black is not.
Black is like the "antagonist Darth Vaders
seduced by the dark side of the Force",
Where whites are always the fairest of them all,
the loveliest and deserving of honors
White meats against black meats.
Are we just referring to the
black trousseaus & black coats with black ties
matching black evening gowns, black fishnets & black sparkling shoes
for galas and formal launches
with the phrase, "black is beautiful"?

Are the white meats superior to the black tissues?
Do you know that the black chickens believed to be a bit of good luck?
Is it the color or the physical looks
that the whites draw a demarcation line between the blacks?
Are blacks less human because of the color of their skin?
It is what emanates from the inside that makes one bad or good.
When the time comes that we will all be leaving this world
Will the whites could still choose who will be with them in heaven?

Taro Footprints
Tono

Upright tree in messy position growing on the roadside field
Seen the leaves ending his life drifting wind in all directions
Mosquito nests are the safest to breed to enjoy the beauty of nature
Taro hits growing hiding in the bushes are rarely used by Insan
Under the grass-covered tree, there were traces of unloading taro

      Dark, lush, and the sun hates the surge
      Still the taro trail slipped along with passionate soul and body
      The black crackle grasped tightly beside the approaching little hoe
      Enchanting taro invites to keep filling the container
      Mosquitoes feast on taro trail with passion

Grass trampled groaning apologies taro trail
Dew bathes footwear without asking in return
Take a step and see a deeply ingrained feeling of humility
Carried with full satisfaction reflected on the face of life
The taro tracks decorate and preserve the natural beauty of God's creation

Ruthlessness or Voidness
Hasan Asy'ari

One day you know
That we are actually the same
The same once resided in the mother's womb

Tomorrow of course we will remain the same
Together they will live in the bowels of the earth

If you think about this
Are you still unconscious
When in fact we are the same
Obliged the same
To love each other
Know each other
Respect also cherishes others

If you still dream about this
We'll still be the same
The right to live the same
Deserve the same treatment

Of course what else
If the small ones are as small as bacteria
Still very useful
Why is that a little because of the color
This has become a differentiator
Aren't we still the same

You're both human

Shadeism
Smruti Ranjan Mohanty

Man is born unique
So different and special
In his own way
Irrespective of social clusters
Caste, creed and colour
Supreme and matchless he is
Having no equal and parallel

The brainchild of man
Delicately nurtured over the years
In the womb of colonialism and imperialism
Colourism and shadeism
Discrimination on the basis of colour
Black, pale and dull
Treating a vast multitude of humanity
Inferior and unacceptable
Is but an attitude of a few
To subjugate others
And convey the message
That they are lesser mortals
Not at par with others
Destined to suffer
For no fault of theirs

Discrimination so apparent
In the fair play of justice
In the field of business, labour,
Housing, healthcare etc.
Hardly there is any space
To breathe in.

Any feeling of superiority
On the basis of colour
Is highly unscientific
Do not have a basis of its own

Men are different
But at par with each other
Each having his own traits
With no one superior or inferior

The wind of change is blowing
With the black people
Proving their worth in every field
And surpassing many
The message is loud and clear
That the days of
Make-believe identities
On the basis of colour
Are but numbered

Let the champions of racism
Realize the reality
That the superiority of races
Are but myths
The world is as much ours
As it is theirs
Time to appreciate the changes
Respect each other's dignity
And make the world
A better place to live in

Children of the Nation
Pepe Wibowo

Since then, my feeling was unable . . .
Imagining my brother's face.
The nation's children lay scattered . . .
Covered with newspapers on the side of the street

The tears of the inhabitants of the sky added to my pity . . .
Even the cold was felt to the ribs . . .
The gaze of a mother who embraces her child . . .
Like a hen that warms up with its wings . . .

The leaders of his nation who looked away at that time . . .
And the angels who are praised blue . . .
Adding to my weak bones.
I wanted to spread my wings to add to the warmth of his body . . .

Oh My God . . .
Is there a gift for a mother's love . . .
Who warmed his child with hunger . . .
Who else would they pity on . . .
Only You can help them . . .

Faintly, I heard the voice of a blind child . . .
Who sang a sweet voice over her suffering . . .
Please . . .
Please help me.
Please help my life . . .
The wind of the stars and the moon . . .
Please Listen to my heart . . .
Please Hear my voice . . .

Oooough . . . I just realized . . .
Isn't this world a place of suffering . . .
Don't I feel it too . . .
Without the taste and greeting of love every day . . .

Stand Up!!!
Noreen Ann Snyder

Let's stop the hatred and violence
against black men, black women and black children.
Let them live in peace and harmony.
It's the government that don't want us
to be united.
They want us all to be divided.
The government wants to destroy
get rid of the blacks. But why?
What have they done wrong?
Nothing, in my book!
Let's put a stop to that.
Let's all get along.
We all want the same thing in life--
to love and to be loved,
family, friends,
education, job, and to help others,
to live in happiness, peace and harmony.
We need to stand together
be united as one as a community
and let the government know
we won't put up with their
bullying the blacks.
They have all the rights
as human beings.
So, let's stand together
and show them who we
really are made out of.

Are you with me?
I can't hear you! Louder!!
Are you with me?
Come on stand up and
let every single person
live in peace, harmony, and happiness.

The Assault upon the Peace of Black Men and Women
Olaoye Olawale Olufemi

When the creator at first made man
He perfected his work; bestowing man with all it takes to be prudential
The advent was without segregation
For all races were encompassed with equality

Ages passes, metamorphosing into new era
Thence, the value dwindled.
Demarcations between races, black discrimination and stigma
Who truncated the onset value?

No freedom for black man oversea
Rights sacrificed as though they're of no importance
Any flaw on the black man skin?
What had spurred the racial discrimination?

Black emigrant can't boast offshore
The sentiment of traveling abroad turned valueless
Since deprival of rights is drastically recurring
Thence; they're allured to admit their stance as inferior

Is the potter who molded all imperfect?
Who can elucidate; the areas comprising flaws?
Blacks deserve fairness and equity as other races
Our stance as dark-skinned deserve utmost regard

Spread round the tidings!
Launch the campaign flag
No to racial discrimination
We're equal; creator's handwork.

I Am Human, Too
Amb Lovelyn P. Eyo

How long shall we . . .
Shall we be blind to humanity
Shall we be deaf to tones of harmony
Shall we be dumb to the words of unity?

The drums of racism you beat erratically aloud
Just to make my voice of innocence drown out
You see me coming
You cast me aside and away
Saying am not worthy
And only need be slain
All because I have done nothing
But only because I am black-
A nobody am marked

I prove competent for the job
Yet my success credentials you lob
Calling for the next white in line
Saying it matters not my life
Because am black and out of line

You say you want peace
But where is thy peace
When you promote the ills?
You can't have it
When you can't keep or nurture it
You say you want peace
But anytime it comes around, away you toss it
By trying to crush me who come in peace into pieces

I did not choose to be black
But bravery and strength chose me
The power to change and restore the world from its lack
Is right inside of me

I Want to Live

Remember I am human too
I deserve to live
Deserve to sustain the world for me and you
Me, you can't create

Only the ALMIGHTY doth make me
So you can't dictate
My existence you can't erase

Our world is only one
Our bond should keep as one
To prosper our progeny
And keep in harmony
Until we all come together
Embracing the hearts of unity further
Then posterity shall live better

Live and Let Live!
Aruna Bose

We are all children of God.
When he never differentiated us
regarding caste, colour or creed,
then who are we to discriminate?

Even nature loves and shares
everything with everyone.
Then why we fight for border lands?
Can't we walk hand in hand?

Our blood is red not blue or black.
Then why so much injustice and inhumanity?
Why love and peace lacks?

Why we are tortured and murdered brutally?
Can't we live happily?
Remember,
United we stand;
Divided we fall.
Come out from narrow walls.

Let's heal the world with
love, peace, unity, equality
and humanity.
Let's pledge for peace and empathy.
Every soul will reach to tranquility.
Let's make a better place to live in.

Between the Sun and the Moon
Andaru Ratnasari, aka Tara Noesantara

From this valley of black slaves to Arizona
When from the hill I looked and heard a sharp screeching
Chest shaking sliced taste

Extensive racial discrimination
When from above the mat I looked . . .
The thunderstorm in the Southeast Ocean
The drums of rebellion sang mourning songs

From this valley Nathaniel Bacon sighed
When the wind hissed past Barkeley
And in longing to swallow time with bullets
The heart melts into doubt
The wind blew shut eyes
Here the sun dies
Only wrenching tears
If you have to die later . . .

Black People's Fighter
Yanz Haryo Darmista

Looking up at the sky black clouds running around
Is a lavender view
The sky was swept blue and dim
The hustle and bustle of the wild night wind
Squirmed an uneasy sigh
Black female slaves were raped
The lonely night stretches out time
Amendments to the legality of slavery
Naked between dark faces looming
The world does not provide perfection
Should I close my eyes to reality
Upheaval between the blacks
Should I be blind
Due to see differences in skin color
Because the world no longer values beauty and honesty
My life is sick with painful wounds
Tensions escalated even more when the Pastors were pressed into political policy
My passion is like fog
Covering physical injuries
When Abraham Lincoln stood at the waist
Everything was silent in the dark
All questions keep secrets . . .

Would My Complexion Ever Matter?
Padmapriya Karthik

If my blackberry-like eyes could
unearth a hidden evidence,
and be a witness to gift justice
to an innocent;

If from my chocolate-coloured lips
kind energy incessantly generates
to console a wounded heart,
counsel a distressed mind;

If my dark-coloured ears grab a listen
to a feeble grief-stricken voice,
and plants hope in the withered soul
as urged by my conscience;

If my ebony-like arms stretch
to distribute alms
and hug the desolate, wrinkled skin,
gifting happiness and warmth;

If from my melanin-rich fingertips
powerful words spark,
and ignite motivation, confidence,
reilluminating the abandoned soul;

If my energetic thoughts are channelized
to irrigate the parched mind with positivity;
and if I play a vital role
to spread love among humanity . . .

Would my complexion ever matter?

Thanksgiving
Monsif Beroual

Skin colors cover the sky
A humankind story that has never used their mind
Neither their heart,
A philosophy of dust inks
Spoke a melody of endless war
But only in thanksgiving we apologize for our fresh history
That never ain't left our mind
Do we really apologize for that broken years?
That we still produce in our children books
Neither into the educational system
We put the poison into inks
Into images to remind them
Skin colors is a sin
And humanity is broken letter, broken to pieces
Still, nowadays we can't bring it together,
Past is gone and the future is coming
The same melody hanging around
Seems humankind never learned
That skin color is a gift, not a sin.

Sower's Ink of Hope
Alicia Minjarez Ramirez

Tactile voices
Bearers of dreams
Fraction – link
The silence.
Cradle semblants
Ebony – ivory
In unison
Of our time.

Vocabulary wrap
The wings of the wind;
Inalienable right,
Universal and intrinsic
Of people.

Dreams inundate words,
Evoke consciences
Without disparity of races.
Sower's inks of hope,
Tolerance and love
Living blood in the marble of life;
As warm breeze sketching
Utopian pilasters,
Aromatic polyphonic incenses,
Seeking transcendence
In memory cavities.

When We Cease All of the Marching . . .
Alonzo Gross

If it were switched,
(Tell me)
How would u feel? /
Would u still bitch,
If for "U" Kaepernick kneeled? /.
What if every day ur people's
Blood would splatter? --
With no regard,
2 ur hard pleas of SCREAMIN'
"WHITE LIVES MATTER!!!" --.
What if?
When u said that,
we laughed more or less/
And said "ALL LIVES MATTER",
Makin A Protest,
2 Yo Protest/
(Oh Yes/) I guarantee,
U would feel it, in yo chest/
The distress/
Of gettin' killed on film
And u gets
no arrest/.
Out of frustration u too,
Would probably riot •
But u'll never "stomach"
What I say,
it's not in ur "diet" •.
Cuz In ur mind,
u think that Everyone favors u /
Like ur Divine,
Truth is . . .
Yer WHITE PRIVILEGE
ENABLES U /

I Want to Live

I think it's time,
U show empathy,
love and respect ----*
Before there comes a time,
We put more than our foots on y'alls necks---.*
Just know I want Peace,
But our gunz is Arching _

So please don't call us Beasts,
When We Cease all of the Marching.

zO

white privilege
hülya n. yılmaz

whites assume me to be one of their own,
though i am a woman born and raised in Turkey
the melanin in my skin is quite light, you see . . .

my birthplace – geographically speaking,
a Eurasian country, gave me a bubble of safety
life was all about parental and sibling love for me there
my extended family contributed to the gentle joys
of many an unforgettable daily affair

not even once did i have the need to tell anyone that i want to live
i just lived, and was let be

Black Turks / Turkish Blacks?
i had not heard about them much,
other than those who were celebrated on stage;
theater actors / actresses and ballet dancers, that is
a true fan of Black musicians i was in my teenage-years

nothing substantial was to be found
in those school books of Turkey's yesteryear
i discovered the centuries-long plight
the Black population endured in the U.S. of A
from a multitude of outside sources in print
and thus, knew way back then
that awareness needed to be raised
for discrimination in any form and shape and to any extent;
not staying silent in the face of injustice and inequality was a must
that none of us should ever allow anyone to willfully pretend
how 'everything is just fine and dandy' while racism is blatantly praised

so, a few pieces of information were gathered
as acquired by this "white" person, privileged at birth
who was objectifying the subject right from the start,
incapable of grasping the brutal reality
which routinely hit Blacks hardest globally

I Want to Live

but hey,
i was ready for an intellectual discussion . . .
what a hypocrisy!

following my formal early education,
i perused several volumes on the Ottoman Empire
the horror of what the Black Eunuchs had to survive
turned for me into a recurring nightmare,
haunting me for many a year
most of them were castrated
when they were assigned to provide
private services in the Harem of the Sultans

i had lived inside a safe bubble, as i said initially
hence, that uncovered segment of the pre-Republic Turkish history
left me in an overpowering shock
such historical accounts had been, after all,
dismissed predominantly all along
it must have been vital to help us, the modern-day Turks,
to continue to proudly gild our precious fame
as a nation of humility,
grace and hospitality . . .

decades later, a name crossed my path:
activist and poet Mustafa Olpak
he was talking about "Dana Bayramı",
"a traditional Afro-Turkish Spring Festival"
at my advanced age, i had come to hear first-hand finally
how Blacks struggled to preserve at least a part of their past
in my otherwise beloved birth-country
some were held as slaves between the 14th and 20th century,
suffering under the Ottoman regime's fire;
others, as Mr. Olpak said, "ascended into rank" within that empire

as we all are aware,
power structures come and go
that is the call
one day, each of them will fall

the oppressed survive them despite it all,
and cultural accounts in the likes of Mr. Olpak's,
thankfully, take hold

still . . .

as a "white" woman of Turkey, i am in despair
because for this horrifying shame, there is no repair

going through all kinds of emotions,
i am desperate to spread the word,
for whatever it might be worth

in my concluding thoughts,
i am reminded of a profound Tolstoy-quote:
"I simply want to live; to cause no evil to anyone but myself."

looking back, way back, as well as viewing my here and now
one dominating fact surrounds my entire life, and it remains intact:
no one 'caused me any evil but myself'

not even once did i have the need to tell anyone that i want to live
i just lived, and was let be

because i am being seen as "a white", you see . . .

But You Did Not Listen, Did You?
William S. Peters, Sr.

Shadows creepin'
Mothers weepin'
Fathers distraught,
Sighing,
Vying,
Denying,
Defying,
What it is

This war has been waged
For over 400 years,
And as Maya once said,
"Still, I rise"

Still, we stand!!!

My eyes have always
Seen clearly
What you have unfairly
Executed
Against
People like me,
People of color
As you methodically
Execute your agendas
To keep 'people like me' . . .
Down

You have laws
That are used
At your discretion . . .
Granting favor to one,
Death to another.

Writers for Humanity

You have a justice system
From the boots on the street
To the prosecutors' offices,
To the court rooms,
To the prisons
That works
To minimalize,
Marginalize
My people

Your education system,
Which is a bias institution
That teaches
Half or non-truths
Has somehow excluded
Our accomplishments . . .
But know this,
"We have done so much with so little for so long,
that we are now capable of doing anything with nothing at all!"

Yes, we can!!!!

I will not address the why,
As to why
You feel threatened
By my presence,
Or why you hate me . . .

Given the opportunity
You actively seek to
Repress me,
And oppress me,
But if you would but
Allow me,
I/We can get my/our own!

I Want to Live

So, let it be known,
There is a sleeping giant,
Who only wanted
To be left alone,
But you kept,
And continue to do
What you do by,
Prodding me/us
And poking,
And stoking the fires
Of our unrest,
Feeding your bias,
To generations to come!

We are yawning loudly,
We are fully awakening,
The crowds of humanity,
Rising as a rainbow,
With all the colors
Expressing a collective unity
That adorns the skies
After the storm

We are not just Black,
And the world, though portrayed
In falsely monochromatic depictions
By decisive idiots, . . .
Shall end

We are a collective humanity
Of many hues
Who refuse
The theosophy of
Eugenicists,
Bigots and Racists
Who say inane and insane things

As I said,
We are awaking,
Forsaking your propaganda,
Tearing the gates and doors
Off of the corrals and cages
That for ages
You have used
To attempt to control
Our souls
. . .

But you cannot,
And you shall learn
The lesson well
As you burn in your own
Private hell . . .

Yes, . . .
You shall learn succinctly,
"Why the caged bird sings"

We warned you,
But you did not listen, did you?
All we ever wished to do
Was LIVE Free

I Want to Live!

Essays, Analyses and Stories

Writers for Humanity

I Want to Live

Mutawaf A. Shaheed, AKA C. E. Shy, has been writing since the seventh grade throughout high school, until he became more involved in sports. After his graduation, this widely published author worked at White Motors Company. "The Poet's Corner", his column in the company's newspaper, constitutes his first publication.

https://www.facebook.com/mutawaf.shaheed

The System
M. A. Shaheed

White supremacy or any other kind of a system that dominates a group or society has a place for everybody who lives in it – thereby creating an unholy alliance to rule over. A constant bombardment of, lies, misdirection, giving the appearance that there many things to be concerned about. All these things emanate from one single source. Using the analogy of an orchestra: it's made up of sections that chime in on command. These commands are planted in the minds of the populace by way of the educational system, entertainment, advertising, the use of force, drugs or habits that bring no benefit to the victims. The victims are always led to believe that some action or inaction by them will change a system that depends on their being gullible and powerless. On every level of that society, there is waiting for the citizens, the second-class overseers, AKA Goons. Any attempt to escape by the victims of their predicament is monitored and squashed by any and all means imagined and made available to the overseers. The very same monitors are themselves victims of the same system. They are as delusional as the people they are appointed over to oppress. They know that if they even think what they are doing is wrong, they will suffer the same fate as the people right under them.

One afternoon, I was with one of my grandsons. He is thirteen years old. We started talking after I got him to relax and open up. During our ride, he asked me why white people hated us so much. He was truly puzzled. I wanted to be as succinct and honest as possible. He has been raised to understand how people are supposed to be, that hate is a negative emotion and has no place in our lifestyle. Additionally, he was confounded, because he wanted to know what we had done to them. I told him that all white people were not like that. I told him there was a type of them that were not human, that they were like monsters. That seemed to clear things up with him, because he sat back in the seat and said in a low voice, "Monsters". He was able to draw the parallel. At his age, he wouldn't be able to understand anything else. As he gets older, he can refine his views and his understanding of that anomaly among the human race. Most likely, it will be easy to figure out who's who, because they will be the same as they have always been. The explanation I gave him was a good starting point. I didn't want to give him the impression that I was trying to soft pedal them or make any kind of excuse for them. He can pass that information to his siblings. This is how I raised his father and his siblings. No delusions to lower their expectations when encountering that entity. Also, in the future, he will be able to recognize monsters and know who or what they are. It gives him a heads-up and shortens the learning curve.

The system can't flourish by just dealing with a minority group; the economy dictates otherwise. It is essential to create false desires and needs in all the people to sustain the energy needed to maintain said system. You will never hear the people in power complain about the system. The oppressed people have appetites unchecked. When talking of the oppressed, you're talking all the people who have no power, who are deluded in believing there are rules to protect them against the status quo. The system is the criminal but can't be punished by the individuals it commits the crimes against. Crime can't sustain the little guy, the persons who have been determined to be the initial targets, the expendables. In reality, there are not too many people that fit that category. What many don't see are the numbers; they mostly see what's around them. The system managers keep a constant eye on the numbers; that includes various incidents accidents, suicides, the list goes on.

There is no perfect man-made system. History proves it over and over. There are only so many stop-gap-measures one can use to fortify it. Every attempt to do so makes things worse. It's like trying to fix the same flat tire 50 times. The same people who built the system are the ones who try and fix it with same intentions as in the first place.

There is enough guilt to spread around. The difference is that there are those whose guilt comes from the pressures of oppression and ignorance, while the architects of the system are ultimately responsible and will carry the burdens that will come with their status. Their denial is what has caused the decease that we as a nation are facing. All the bystanders are and have always been culpable in the crimes and the sickness that has resurfaced in the nation. Like any virus that goes untreated, it spreads and mutates. In this writer's opinion, it's beyond control because of the system we have participated in and ignored. Whatever the individual thinks or believes, you can't un-ring a bell. It is a system, and a people who are recalcitrant. They think of their acts of murder and genocide are somehow patriotic – a place where hatred is managed and manipulated to the benefit of the benefactors. The people have lost, or never had a shred of decency. As a result, we are all suffering. We are all participants and victims of a malignant system, built on another system of the same kind. Too many holes in the dykes.

A Place That Hate Ate
M. A. Shaheed

There are expectations by some that America will pay black people reparations for what they did to them in a documented history of slavery in the USA. That would be saying that the mistreatment and murder of blacks have come to an end. That the government has done all that is/ was necessary to ensure that the inhumane treatment has come to an end. The question is, how could anyone arrive at a figure when you are trying to address something that has not stopped? It is no different than saying that in order to travel at a certain speed and cover long distances in a short period of time in space is to bend it in half. Where is the middle when it continues to expand?

Additionally, how could they explain that it to make sense to the white groups that have done their bidding for centuries? The promise has been that they would never allow blacks to be higher in the society than whites; no matter how dumb, illiterate or insane they are or get to be. How would they compensate them for helping to maintain the status quo of racism and white supremacy? Where is their money going to come from? They have gone above and beyond board to do what was asked of them.

You can see presently the state of affairs with this administration in the White House. Those people feel betrayed by the former managers of the status quo. They want to be rewarded for their past performance. It is already at a fever pitch as we speak. To even suggest giving black people anything without giving the loyal racists more would surely be a catastrophe. Hate is one of the more important management tools used to maintain order. It's a kind of glue used to hold a racist nation together. They, the powers that be, know if they gave black people money or anything that would be considered equal or more, it would revert back to them in a matter of weeks. Everything they would spend it on would have little to no impact to a community that is as divided as black folks. They don't have a community or leadership or factories that produce anything; so, the money would go back to the coffers to the white business right away. In fact, they would be further in debt than before. The things they purchased would be repossessed and confiscated. The question is how could they justify it to 100 million + racists? So, they just sit and watch the people run their mouths in anger, calmness or rant and rave, whatever mode they choose to express themselves. At the end of the day, they have the guardians of their freedom, the police. That has always been the first and last resort. They have been empowered by the supreme court to do whatever they need to do in order to show the people that might makes right. I find it amazing that black people are still expecting these people to respond to them any differently than they have ever responded. If the god that they made up for themselves were to come down from where they have him at and said he would forgive them for every crime that they ever committed, if they would stop now, they would tell him to go on back to where he came from, because, not only can they not stop, but he can't stop them.

As an African American in this nation, you have absolutely no rights at all. It's always been you or them and the nation was set up for them. They have made up lies to make themselves feel superior to black people. It has been done through all available outlets. These people can't afford to have remorse, a conscience that kind of emotion undermines the very fabric of the nation. Those feelings are foreign. This place was not set up on those principles. There are so many facets to racism, it can be written about and discussed over and over again and never touch on the same points. The catalyst is hatred; the rest falls into place automatically. Racism has its rules, immigrants must follow those rules or suffer the consequences for challenging the way of life in America. There are organizations that have been funded and designated to be the conduits for all immigrants entering the US. Their job is to incorporate these people into the ways of the cultural life of the country – the dos and don'ts of the society.

    The success of the nation didn't come from being like that. The benefits have come from being the very opposite. I have a good friend who is a writer and an attorney. He thinks that somehow, if you just tweak the system a little, things will be better for all involved. My assertions are as follows: it won't happen because it can't happen, because of a people who lack courage on every level of human dignity to stand up to the forces of evil. You can call that evil or by whatever name you choose. It is at the very core of our society, run by those who have been chosen, or if you will, elected to what the foundations of the country was established for. If anyone stands in the way of that, they will be eliminated in some way. They are arranged in ranks to deal with any attempts foreign or domestic to change anything that doesn't fit the bill. It's a shell game, sleight of hand. Why would some create more competition for themselves and their grandchildren, when they have gone through so much effort to get rid of it? They have encouraged the maligning and slaughter of thousands upon thousands of black men, women and children to that desired end. They have done everything possible to make sure blacks couldn't compete then and now. They have established middle management on every part of the nation to ward off the ambitions of black folks, to arrest, fine and disable them. The potential the nation has had available to be self-sufficient has been dulled by a voracious appetite for racism and un justified hatred.

    The people who could be trained to be doctors, engineers, scientists within our own country are not encouraged by the deranged or among the racist elements in high places. To the effect that they import those professionals from other parts of the world. What has made itself manifest during this plague are the shortages created by such behavior. It could have been avoided. Cutting off one's nose to spite one's face is surely a sign of an ignorant beast. It will be the continued mismanagement of these very assets through the mental illness of racism that will be the undoing of this nation, any nation. An old friend told me a long time ago, "the only way a person can know your pain is to feel it themselves." Anyone that would pray for the continuation of their pain is sicker than those who inflict it. It matters not what party occupies the seats of power; blacks will continue to be the life of the parties, no matter what they promise. That should be obvious by now.

Writers for Humanity

I Want to Live

Born and raised in Brooklyn, NYC, Shareef Abdur-Rasheed, AKA "Zakir Flo", is a Vietnam era veteran, human rights activist and a percussion artist. He writes conscious poetry and socio-political commentaries, has authored Poetic Snacks 4 the Conscious Munchies and contributed to numerous international anthologies. Shareef is married with 9 children, 44 grandchildren and 4 great grandchildren.

https://www.facebook.com/shareef.abdurrasheed1
https://zakirflo.wordpress.com
http://www..com/shareef-abdur-rasheed.php

Oh Mankind, There Is No Such Thing as Races!
A Message to All Mankind
Shareef Abdur-Rasheed

The creator of Mankind (not Human race) from one man (Adam, aws) and one woman (Howa/Eve, aws), and from them, made Mankind into nations and tribes that we may know one another for identity, variety just like other creation, animals, flowers, etc. – not to despise one another (Qur'an: Al-Hujurat :49,13). It goes on after stating that in the verse that in and of itself is not what concerns Allah as important by revealing "The most honorable among you are those who have piety, Taqwa (fear and obey thee creator). The concept of "Race" is a tool of Shaitan to divide Mankind and create fitnah (mischief, mayhem, etc.) on Earth; it is from Men affected by that tool in their ethnic, national, tribal arrogance and pride, one nation or tribe looking down on the other as inferior, creating fear, hate, suspicion, including wars and killing each other. The word alone, "Race", wreaks of evil divisiveness. Think for a moment even if you describe Mankind as "Human Race" that all humans belong to, then how could there be other races if everyone already is a member of the Human Race? Don't you see how senseless that is? Unfortunately, Mankind of all tribes and nations have not escaped being fooled by this evil plot that has evolved into a deadly disease that has torn Mankind apart. Mankind continues to buy into this lie. It behooves us to step back a moment and think about this deeply. This is serious! We must reshape our thinking in accordance with what the Creator revealed as his definition of his creation, "Mankind". May the Creator of all living things instill in us all the genuine concern to love and unite the entire humanity as one and ferociously fight all ignorance that the Shaitan uses to lead us astray from the guidance of the Creator of all living things from the very first creation. The giver and taker of life. Ameen!

I Want to Live

Some Things Pertaining to
White Institutional Racism in America Today
End of 2020, Entering 2021
Shareef Abdur-Rasheed

Considering: Africans were brought here by way of being captured, abducted, kidnapped, forced into slavery to perform slave labor in a far-off land, thousands of miles from mother Africa; jammed into the belly of ships in the most inhumane, deplorable, demeaning way, laying in their own waste, chained, shackled, packed like sardines often next to someone who died along the way and left until finally deposited in the sea, creating an extremely toxic, diseased environment brought about by Slavers in the business of capturing, selling human cargo in large quantities, delivering them once reaching various destinations from the Islands in the Caribbean to the North American Continent mainland . . . that brings with it a reality that is rarely addressed. Again, Africans were forced to be here in slavery. They were not considered citizens, fellow countrymen and women, neighbors, comrades, etc. but slaves to be bought and sold. Regardless, that history says the so-called negros were freed, given freedom on Jan. 01, 1863. They were then and right now to this day considered in a way as though Africans were never set free; because in reality, Africans were never set free in a pure sense, not even close. It's like an ex-con who can't get a job because he's an ex-con. Yes, he/she paid their debt to society but most won't hire them as if they're not ex-cons but in fact still cons. You know, 'once a ---- always a---- kind' of thing. The only difference is, conceivably one can lie about who actually did time and conveniently fail to disclose it. It's not likely that anyone can hide their being black, except in a relatively few instances. In a society, where you are stigmatized by the color of your skin to the point that it impacts on your quality of life, or in fact, to the point of life and death, that's one hell of a problem that leads to the cry, "I just want to live." I mean, are you supposed to apologize for living? Well excuse me! HOODS!

     So, they got special places for black and brown folk, especially in AmeriKKKa. They're called hoods, ghettos. They are overwhelmingly of an inferior quality of life; for example, in crimes, addiction, lack of goods, services, sub-par living conditions as well as education, inflated prices for poor quality goods, etc. Quality crops need a healthy environment to grow. If they're not in an environment that enhances growth, they wither and die; so do humans. Therefore, in an adverse, deprived environment that are death traps, they're set up to fail in life. And who is better to underscore that than racist cops trolling your hood with guns and badges looking to put you in the grave ASAP, acting not just as judge and jury, but as executioner. That brings something to mind. When the so-called (never saw one like the white sheets on my bed) white folk say, when the discussion is slavery or the lynching of black folk, "That wasn't me way back then; why should I feel guilty or held accountable?" I'll tell you why: there are a very significant number of citizens who identify as white Americans who wholeheartedly support those cops who murder black folk to this very day without any probable cause. At the very least, you always have been silent, and when the system played that systemic Racism tune, you dance to it. You are racist to the core and a hypocrite who are no different from your ancestors. Your very silence constitutes collusion with those who fire the bullets into the bodies of innocent human beings or conspire systematically to condemn black, brown, people of color into lives of oppression with little hope of rising up and out of a dismal existence in poor living conditions, sub-par education, zealous, over aggressive occupation force policing, never to protect and serve but to murder, maim, imprison being the prime objective. Your definition of crime is "Blacks, Latinos, etc." – people of color. Y'all vote for bigot politicians to support the continuation of oppression of black and brown citizens whom you never accepted as equal but instead as low lives, dem others, those people, and slaves. You have a president who is your poster boy for white supremacy, though he is also a pathological liar, sociopath, criminal, mass murderer, supported by a party who ignores that, remains silent and supports him anyway and allows him to be above the law so that his supporters in their districts don't vote them out of office.

Ghettos were set up in Europe by Hitler's Nazi Party to isolate people from the general population and earmark them for extinction. If a society is humane and endowed with vast wealth, there should never be hoods, ghettos, or any homeless people. That is the actions of those who are inhumane, hateful, greedy, arrogant, and evil. It's supposed to be "high tide lifts all boats". Therefore, an inclusive society must want the best for all its citizens. A chain is only as strong as its weakest link. AmeriKKKa is not great. AmeriKKKa is sick.

I Want to Live

Born in the turbulent 60s in Mississippi, Gail Weston Shazor grew up in both the deltas of the south and the concrete of Chicago. The mother of three and Gram to two, her desire is to continue to write and to send her words wherever they will go.

I Want to Live . . .
Gail Weston Shazor

And live well.
And without fear.

Without the tiredness brought on by being black and living black . . . all day.

There is a tradition in Southern-rooted black families of attending Watch Night service on New Year's Eve. I have attended many services that began somewhere around 10PM that lasted well after midnight. I grew up believing that everyone went every year to their respective churches for this service. It wasn't until I attended a diverse high school when I learned that not only did other races and religions not practice Watch Night service, they had never heard of it.

    This particular service has morphed into a quasi-religious one in churches in our community. The celebration of Watch Night service began as one marking the anticipation of the Proclamation of Emancipation going into effect on January 1, 1863. Living in near slavery days, keeping watch was also essential for safety. Shooting weapons to welcome in the new year has long been a tradition in the United States. Shooting people during mass weapon fire has also been a tradition. The "throw a rock and hide your hand" practice is easily hidden during mass firing. Families gathered in the church, a safe haven and often considered hallowed ground, to wait out the gunfire and decrease the possibility of murder by white hands.

    The year 2020 has been a challenging one for everyone. The health pandemic none withstanding, black and brown people across the world have been victimized in every aspect of their lives. There is no need to look for statistics, because we live the numbers daily. We die faster and more than anyone else. The current presidential administration embraces the idea that we are somehow in need of oppression and marginalization when it is in fact the inherited privilege that bespeaks for control of their own lives. The dominance of others keeps the pressure of real change and acceptance far off the radar. Fear mongering has resurged into the mainstream. Over and again, history has taught us that fear coupled with hate equals death.

    I have a black and brown body. My children and grandchildren have black and brown bodies. I live on an island mostly peopled with black and brown bodies. I worry that the next news entry will contain the details of the demise of more black and brown bodies and I fear that it will be someone I love.

I Want to Live

I rarely feel safe. I navigate this world on a wire. The vulnerability of the skin I am in and my femaleness is a combination that I find difficult to move through daily. While I celebrate my talents and my intelligence, it is exactly that which has left me alone for many years. The aloneness is something that we rarely speak about, yet it affects every aspect of our personal and professional lives. It also makes women a greater target for racism, sexism, ageism and any other ism you can think of.

Today, I am tired from living Black. Today I am tired from living Native. This does not make me paranoid, it makes me wary. On December 31, 2020, I will sit Watch Night in my house, still waiting on my emancipation, knowing that even the law will continue to fail me. Tomorrow, the things that went bump in this night will be fully visible in the street.

Writers for Humanity

I Want to Live

Penn State Emerita, hülya n. yılmaz is a multi-lingual author, literary translator, and Co-Chair and Director of Editing Services at ICPI. Her poetic work has appeared in approximately one hundred and sixty anthologies of global endeavors. hülya finds it vital for everyone to understand a deeper sense of self, and writes creatively to attain a comprehensive awareness for and development of our humanity.

https://hulyanyilmaz.com/

Even an Off-White Person Has White Privilege
hülya n. yılmaz

I was born and raised in Turkey. My immediate environment provided me with a safe bubble. Then came a time, when my parents, my brother and I lived in Germany for several years. As a stipend-earned scholar in a prominent research institute, my father had a respectable status there – unlike other 'marginal', i.e., non-German people. We could afford as nice of a single-family house as any of the Germans living in the same neighborhood. In other words, we had considerable privilege as the 'non-mainstream' residents of that country.

Before the first year I was going to attend a German school at the age of ten, my parents wanted to help get me used to being on my own outside our home-setting. They sent me to a nearby store to pick up a few items one afternoon. Other customers were there. All blond and blue-eyed. The cashier asked me one question: "Warum sind deine Augen so schmutzig?" / "Why are your eyes so dirty?" He then added: "Wäschst du sie nicht?" / "Don't you wash them?" I have brown hair and brown (well, Hazel) eyes. On the way home, I cried. I didn't hide my tears from my parents when I got home. I told them what had happened. They showed their sadness silently at first. Only later on did they give me a few pointers as to how I could respond to the potential of similar comments. My favorite was: "I love chocolate. So, my eyes have the color of chocolate." (I really do love chocolate.) Dad added some other humorous 'comebacks' to my repertoire. I felt well-equipped as far as protecting my feelings from getting hurt.

I studied very hard in that German school. I was a star student in Turkey, but worked considerably harder in Germany because I obviously was going to be singled out among my 'pure-blood' German peers; so much so that I became our primary teacher's best student. Dear Mr. Hetzsche! He had only one leg, having lost the other one in the war. He might have been even one of the Hitler Youth members. Whatever his past life may have been like, he never allowed xenophobia disturb my presence to any degree. (Btw., "xenophobia" within the German context is a concept that I understood many years later.) In composition class one day, we had to write a brief impromptu essay. I completed mine first. When everybody was done, we started reading our assignments out loud. For my work, I earned the highest grade. A girl and a boy from across my chair shouted to Mr. Hetzsche that I had cheated. Dear, dear, dear man! I will never forget that kind soul who always showed me his heart's tenderness. He knew as well as I did that there was no cheating done from my end. His response still filled me with confidence and pride: "I have been watching all of you very carefully. Hülya didn't move her head away even once from the blank paper I gave each one of you. You two, however, were fidgeting in your seats, looking around during the entire hour. I'll see you both after class."

I Want to Live

The first Christmas came around. I was selected as one of the angels for the season-specific school play. My parents told me much later that several parents complained to the school administration about having a brown-haired, brown-eyed Christmas Angel on stage. In that evening, Dad told me their story from their stay in Munich when my brother and I were toddlers. My parents were renting a flat in an apartment building near the Olympic Stadium. The kitchen was shared by all tenants on each floor. Not speaking German very well, Mom was always uneasy about being alone with us while Dad was in his office a little far away. Mom had just cooked our lunch and was on her way back to our flat. The landlady rushed out of her home, unleashing her dog and signaling him toward Mom. Mom was terrified of dogs. Before that day. Much more so afterward. Once Dad talked with that woman after work, he concluded that she was trying to get us out of there in order to make room for tenants whom she could charge a considerably higher rent. It was, after all, time for the Olympic games to begin.

Decades later, the U.S.A. happened, when I, in pursuit of my doctoral degree, applied to The University of Michigan. In the department, I was the only 'foreigner' amid blond-haired, blue-eyed German and American students. All of the German professors, with the exception of one, treated me as an unwanted outsider. For them, I represented 'this woman' from a backward Muslim nation. Not German. Not American. Just an "Oriental" (yes, I was referred to as being from an oriental country). In grading my assignments and term papers, the German faculty was routinely harsh. Unfoundedly harsh. One incident, particularly, stands out as a still unsettling memory. It was toward the end of my first semester, when I found out that my mother was critically ill. She had developed cancer prior to my leaving Turkey, was transferred to have a second surgery in Germany after the first one was in vain as far as the metastasis. One professor in whose seminars we had to write a semester-end research paper refused to give me an "Incomplete" grade. The department had no policy whatsoever when the doctoral students' requests for incomplete grades were concerned. He flat out told me that I would fail his course and would have to take it again for an entire semester (there was a deadline for course completion regarding the Ph.D. programs; none of us had multiple years to depend on). The department head interfered on my behalf, which helped me acquire the "incomplete" grade.

After eight hours in my overseas flight, throughout which I agonized over the condition of Mom, I finally was at the passport check counter. The minute the employee who handled my entry forms saw my passport and stamped it with an obvious disgust on his face, he threw it to the floor. I had no U.S. citizenship back then. Turks, the largest and the economically highest contributing minority in Germany, were back then and are still on Germans' radar of prejudice, stereotyping and rejection. After I returned from my trip to Mom's death, that German professor didn't even have one nice thing to say to me upon my delivery of my term paper.

Have I been chastised because of the way I look? Yes. Have I been subjected to stereotyping and prejudice on the basis of my ethnic background? Yes. Still, not even once did I have the need to assert the obvious; namely, that I want to live. I lived and I was let be. White privilege? Most certainly!

Can any of the discriminatory or condescending treatments I was subjected to, of being singled out or chastised, be equated to what my fellow humans go through since the day they were born with darker melanin in their skin? Absolutely not! What an absurd comparison one such would make!

Professor Barnor Hesse in the Department of African American Studies at Northwestern University offers an eye-opening treatise in a list, "The 8 White Identities": 1. White Supremacist, 2. White Voyeurism, 3. White Privilege, 4. White Benefit, 5. White Confessional, 6. White Critical, 7. White Traitor, and 8. White Abolitionist. His analysis of "whiteness" led me to some much-needed soul-searching – although I may only be considered an "off-white" individual. #1 is an identity even my enemies could not equate me with. The same holds true for #2. I have, however, been granted the 3rd and the 4th identities throughout my life. #5 does not relate to me by any stretch of the imagination – that of my own included. Assuming that I have understood #6 of Professor Hesse's scholarly argument correctly, I have always been critical of whites, including myself, and I never shy away from speaking up on the false narratives white people are adamant about disseminating with a willful and passionate disregard of historical accounts, fear, blind hatred, and lack of introspection. If #7 and #8 are to be taken as being a traitor to and opponents of white supremacists and / or whites who are under their ludicrous conviction that only their lives matter, then I represent both of those identities – and proudly so. Earlier, I had said that I didn't even once have the need to assert my birthright; namely, the fact that I want to live. Why then should Blacks ever have to articulate the same right? That we all want to live is not open for a discussion.

I Want to Live

William S. Peters, Sr., aka 'Just Bill', is an award-winning global activist for humanity. His poetry and prowess have been acknowledged and translated across the world. He is the founder and chair of Inner Child Enterprises, Inner Child Press International and the World Healing, World Peace Foundation. He utilizes these vehicles along with his poetry and other writings to champion the cause of consciousness, peace, love, acceptance and compassion. His personal perspective is that 'life is a garden', and we must plant seeds of good intent, light and love that we all may harvest a sweet bountiful fruit. The 'by-line' Mr. Peters has coined for Inner Child Press International is 'building bridges of cultural understanding'. Achieving this vital connection is his inspiration.

I Will Not Go Quietly into the Night!
William S. Peters, Sr.

When i was a child of about 2–3 years of age, i had the opportunity to go to town with my grandmother, endearingly known as "Grandma 'ouise" (pronounced "Wees" short for Louise). My self being the only child at that time, i was doted on with much love and celebration. You see, both of my parents were somewhat orphaned and only children. They were raised by someone other than their "natural" parents. i [sic] was so loved, being the first-born. There was nothing i did not have, want for or needed.

Well, on this occasion, we went to town on a typical Saturday morning. This was a very exciting time for a young child, especially one as precocious as myself. When we arrived in the town, which i will not mention, we went to the local super store. A "Super Store" at that time was an exciting adventure. They had food items, snacks, toys, clothing, and most of all, people . . . Different people of all types, shapes, colors, sizes, etc. . . . This was truly a treat for a young curious mind such as mine. They even had a soda fountain!

To set up this scenario . . . i spent a couple of years after my birth in the South. Having been born in Philadelphia, Pennsylvania, my mother traveled back to her home for family support. My father was overseas in the Korean War, and my mother was a cute, young 20-year-old female in a city that she knew not and where she was alone. So, going back South to her family home, a familiar setting, was "safe".

Anyway, in the store, i was in a world of wonder . . . i still have this picture of excitement embedded in my spirit. Being the energetic and hyper type of young boy i was, my grandma, of course, kept me on a very tight leash, figuratively speaking. This was a "South" of 1953 . . . a place where it was clearly evident that people had their "place", retrospectively speaking. As a natural explorer of life with an eye full of wonder and a mind full of questions, i did not know of this premise; and quite frankly, i am not sure that i would have acquiesced, if i did. Georgia was a unique state back then than it is now . . . it has quite a bit of color to its demeanor.

So, in the store, i discovered that in our journey there was a place where people sat down: a "soda counter" . . . and of all wonders, the seats were round and they spun around. WOW! This was probably the first time i ever saw such a contraption . . . i was smitten and taken! Somehow, i managed, quite cleverly i must say, to escape the close quarters of my grandma's watchful eye and made my way to this "personal merry-go-round"; i excitedly climbed aboard and took my place in the most ultimate of glee on my quixotic adventure. The elderly lady behind the counter looked at me and smiled in a somewhat quizzical manner, which i later came to understand as . . . who knows? At that age, any one adult was elderly.

I Want to Live

Anyway, my grandma spotted me and quickly came over and said: "Boy, get down from there!" Of course, me being the adventurous, curious explorer of life and knowledge that i am, i simply asked: "Why?" i [sic] don't quite remember being given an adequate explanation then or at a later time, but i had no other choice but to obey; for my grandma hurriedly lifted me of with an apology to the lady behind the counter. This went by me like a marble snowball rolling down Everest. But what did strike me and thus left an indelible impression upon my young curious mind to this day was the dubious reply from the lady behind the counter . . . and that was: "He must not be from around here!"

To this day, i will not dignify the meaning by an inane explanation of what was meant, nor will i acknowledge, hopefully never, that there are lines drawn in our experiences that separate me and you. But i will say this: it is up to me as to whether i embrace these predetermined limits on myself or not, and i will not go quietly into the night!

Writers for Humanity

Voices Behind the Wire

Writers for Humanity

I Want to Live

Introduction

This section of this anthology, *I Want to Live*, is especially important we believe, for it includes voices of individuals from the 'other side'. What I mean about the 'other side' is that the authors of the following writings are incarcerated, and thus separated from 'mainstream' society. These individuals many times must suffer the indignities, cruelties and other 'human' brutalities we exact upon each other.

I felt that their voices were significant, for they provide a perspective of "I Want to Live" that is unique because of their circumstances. I will not go any further in prefacing the following works and words. I will allow you to interpret and be the judge of the worthiness of listening.

Bless Up

Bill

Nightmares into Dreams
Shaylor Watson

MARCH 7, 1987, MY NIGHTMARE BEGAN.
NOT KNOWING THAT I WAS GOING TO LOSE
FAMILY,
ASSOCIATES,
FRIENDS.

A (18) YEAR OLD KID IN MY COUNTY JAIL BLUES.
DIDN'T KNOW ANYTHING ABOUT JAIL BUT WHAT'S SEEN
ON THE NEWS.

IN SCHOOL I DID LEARN THAT HARRIET TUBMAN, FREED SLAVES
HOWEVER SYSTEMS FED SMOKE.
SHIMMERING MIRAGES LEADING TO EARLY GRAVES.

YET
NIGHTMARES CAN BECOME DREAMS,
REGARDLESS OF WHAT YOU HAVE SEEN.

TOGETHER, IN HERE, EVERYONE ACCOMPLISHES MORE.
WHEN HYPOCRISY DOESN'T GET CONFUSED WITH DEMOCRACY.

WHERE NOT ONLY SOME BLACK LIVES MATTER,
BUT ALL BLACK LIVES MATTER.

WHERE YOUR CHARACTER IS NOT DEFINED BY CASTE OR CLASS.
BUT THE INTEGRITY OF BLACKNESS,
MADE APPARENT THROUGH HUMANITY IN REVOLT

WHAT IS SHARED WITH OTHERS IS NOT GLUT FOR THE SELF
I WANT NO MORE BLACK SUFFERING. NO MORE
SYSTEMIC PAIN. NO MORE
SENSELESS SHOOTINGS OR WARMONGERS GAMES. NO MORE

I Want to Live

CHILDISH GAMES IN HEARTLESS STREETS. NO MORE
LIVES LOST TO THE FASCISM OF LAW OR PANDEMIC. NO MORE
STEALING FROM EACHOTHER, TERRITORIAL KILLINGS.
BLACK WOMEN SUBJUGATED BY TROUBLED MEN. NO MORE

AFTER (32) YEARS OF BEING A PAWN IN THE SCHEME,
I TAKE CONTROL OF THIS SCENE

TURNING NIGHTMARES INTO DREAMS   .

Feel (for) Me?
Ben "Solo" Martinez

Black lives matter,
Black lives matter

I wonder, however, does my life matter?
I assume that most, would
likely respond with a resounding "no!"
Especially considering the pace of your
Existence and the path of your pursuits.
How could you? Even begin to recognize,
When it's clear, that you couldn't care less.
The definition of selfish, perched
Precariously on the balcony of your ivory
Tower. In complete denial of the life and
Path that was chosen long ago for the

Divine you.
But don't get mad,
Be glad that you're receiving the real.

Maybe now your subconscious is
Ready for a little truth, that just might
Rattle and shake somethin' loose
And challenge your existence, in a positive
And good way, because most of us are
Waiting to be reconnected with our descendants
And long-separated family, feel me?

Let's hope so, cause the truth I'm spittin'
Has just begun. So lemme Bless you with
A little Divine Law . . . All things are intimately
Connected, including "You" and "I"

And who am I? Well, that's a bit
Complex, with many layers of subtext, so
Lemme just brush the surface and say that I'm
A worthy, enlightened, conscious Black man,
Who's acquired a good understanding of
Humanity's divinity and purpose.

I Want to Live

My heart and love are great, and
Through my perception, I'm able to acknowledge
And embrace your life and offer that your
Life matters as well.

It is, in this spirit, that I implore
You to open your eyes and begin to do the work
Of weeding out the flaws and contradictions
In your mind, heart and spirit, in search of
Greater empowerment and connectivity.
I need you

Black lives in/of crisis
Been for quite some time now . . .

The lingering effects of humanity lost.
Still existing and flourishing, in new
And modern forms, to this day.
Requiring a genetic change, on the cellular level,
So that the ones who follow are enlightened and conscious from
The Divine food, stacked on life's shelves
For our spiritual nourishment . . .

Black lives do matter . . .
All Black lives matter . . .

I invoke the Black, because you've lost the connection
And chose untruth. So, until you awake,
My non-African Brotha's and Sista's, and recognize the turmoil ablaze
On your doorstep and finally embrace the Divine power you hold,
Towards being a link in the ultimate solution of peace, unity
And love realized, I'll be shakin' the foundation
With this voice, shouting

ALL BLACK LIVES MATTER! Feel me?

My Government, Tis' of Thee
Charles Baker

Zoot suited and combat booted
Khaki uniformed; creased and stiff from heavy starch
Black flags flying lazily in the wind
Violated by every last one of the Cardinal sins
While we're considered an abomination by society
Military branch being of the all-Hood variety
Denied and unrecognized by our own government
But I bet they can count every house in my Hood with a family
    to be evicted because they're unable to make rent
Every shell from them noise makers that my enemies have ever sent
Every soul that lost their lives in the hood where their last
    moments were spent
Eyes closed; head bowed; hands clasped in prayer; knees bent
Every week it seems we're caravanning to another funeral
Government still acting as if we don't exist
Plausible deniability as if we're Black Ops
If the truth was to ever unfold, I don't think that the true
    number could ever be told
How many black lives have been executed by both black and white cops?
All of a sudden black lives matter
After an eternity of Black lives, Black families, and Black culture being shattered
To protect and serve?
However, how many have seen their unfair share of Black lives with
    Their brains splattered
Casualties of calamities and we're still being denied
When asked why . . . guess what?
The government lied
Born subconsciously military minded
Every time a shot's heard, it's likely the government's behind it
They're moving forward; steadily progressing
And it seems our movement is being rewind
Stressing . . . damn, depressing
Words spoken, saying one thing and doing another
Fuck what they said because their actions define it
Didn't I just say our movements being rewinded?
For no other reason than being Black
A perceived threat to their presumed superiority
My enemies are those that for no real reason want me dead

I Want to Live

Recorded and called it history
But that's their story so fuck what you read
Systematically killing us
Not a Holocaust, though many Black lives have also paid that cost
On intimate terms with both Harris and Ross
Casualties and calamities, and I know plenty of Black lives lost
Enlisted as a kid and militarized
When it rains it pours
But when a mother loses her child to these street wars . . .
She cries
I represent very hood and for every hood I'm a soldier
On my back [for my Blackness] I carry every hood on my shoulders
The assaults that have been committed against
In return my pen and ink wages war
For those that tried to abandon the Hood, (AWOL) absent without leave
Foolishly believing they're exempt from participating in this unholy war
Shocked that the government is still ignoring your nigger pleas
(Sppsh) Nigga please
All of a sudden because Obama served (8) eight Black lives matter?
After an eternity of Black lives, Black families, and Black culture being shattered?
Now trumped by Trump who speak of building a wall
But in every Hood, I know some walls that have long since existed
And every life within has long since been restricted
Openly spewing hate to and for the unseen hand and an invisible oppressor
    who so happens to be clearly seen
Who's well aware of every family that can't make rent
Who deserves every shell in their direction that has even been sent
Loving my ghetto's where the government's time has rarely been spent
And the census keeps count of lives lost and where life's last moments were spent
Seems like every week I'm going to another funeral
Zoot suited and combat booted
Khaki uniformed; creased and stiff from heavy starch
Backwards we march
Eyes closed; head bowed; hands clasped in prayer; knees bent
Fully aware of where the rent money went

My Mantra:

"Fuck the government"
My government, tis' of thee
Falsified by a supremacist sense of white liberty
Eyes open and it's clear to see
My government's really my enemy

Scorched Earth
Ras'safidi

Why are there so many Black Folks in a cell?
Why is it a crime to promote a Black man's Heaven,
And curse the white man's Hell?

Why is it so disgraceful to consider one's self Afrikan?
Minus the AmeriKKKans who corrupted the Morrigan's chapter.
No place exists of the German Fascist Pasture.
Neo-Nazi Black Supremacist in support of rebuilding Mussolini's Castle.

What the hell is Ghetto Buji?
We in disguise or in the skies.
Don't trade the youth for Roman lies, or
Promissory Notes to Celtic Gods.
A chosen people who've been set aside,
Rule the earth un-identified.

If Black Lives Matter
Where are we foster childs?
Why are we fosters child?
Who flipped the switch of Yosef's Bey
And turned us into the lost and found?
Why not consider us Shia Sufi, or
Islamic Hebrew of the Nile?

If the twelve tribes have a daughter tribe,
And the thirteenth stands alone,
Is there fourteen cylinders of the Nubian Parameters
Shaded away over in Rome?

If Black Lives Matter
Who runs the Vatican?
Industry? Or Aliens?
Whose alliance protects our interest?
Two Pigmy or Chalk-Asians?
Black liberation, or
White integration?
What's the quickest way to get our land?
Maintaining a dying planet, or

Repatriation to the Motherland.

If Black Lives Matter
Why preserve White nursery rhymes?
Why spread white lies to children's minds
Through public schools and welfare lines?
Why shave black heads and perm black hair, then blame us for blurring the lines.
Yes, black is beautiful but what does it matter if WE withhold
What WE are inside.

Skulls and bones, mortgaged home,
Federal grants and corporate loans.
Private postal shipping services,
Roll-over fees and bridging tolls.
The unknown mark of the supreme alphabet,
Made known by the solar stone.
Lifted and never anchored out,
Resurrected as the Uni-cone.

Dreadlocks from my head rock
Spread wise and send down rays.
One lock alone occupies a space
That guides our nations beyond this age.
Inherited gift of divinity
Calculating using ancient scales.
Intuitive nature exploring primitive
Beginnings mystified by militant Maoist
Berber cells.

If Black Lives Matter
Where's the commitment to make it real?
Why negotiate with anti-black radicals as a means
To re-invent the international banking wheel?
Occupy Wall Street under the table with the
N.O.I? What the hell you got in 'yo EYE?
Fellow guy of Nimarä.
A stolen legacy, or bleached culture.
A rogue nation of stowaways.
Broken treaties, abandoned charters.
A summoned spirit outside the way.

I Want to Live

Can You . . .
Anthony Hawk Hoskins

Excuse me Miss, but can you see me through these walls of concrete and steel bars,
Can you understand my words as they pass through a dead man's world.
Shattering souls, rebelling minds, whispers of hope, screams of times gone by.
Excuse me Miss, why do you laugh, as I stand in the midst of loneliness and despair.

      Can you see me, can you feel me, Miss?

This tightly grasp pouch contains visions, tears, as well as hopes and fears.
I see this reality, I feel so much of its pain, but I refuse to submit to man's proclaimed
Destiny, or shed the slightest amount of self-shame.

      Can you see me, can you feel me, Miss?

Labeled as an outcast from society, a society who rejected me before birth.
The society, who embraced me as I entered into an institution of madness, slavery and hurt.

      Can you see me, can you feel me, Miss?

Housed by the controlling forces, as they force their force on the weak and confused,
Shit this could be you too.
      Why are you laughing, can you see me, can you feel me, Miss?
Searching through pebbles of life on a sandy beach, armed with nothing but
Mixed-up hopes and twisted dreams.
Fixated on easy come-up's, while choosing your sacrificial runner-up's.

      Can you see me, can you feel me, Miss?

Trapped by policies, guns and guards. Who would shoot me just because I look like one of
The lost boys. Who couldn't be freed from these sad set of bars and closed drawers.

      Can you see me, can you feel me, Miss?

Bedrocks of racism galvanized through vast forms of media, pushed through
Institutions of miseducation and religions.
Prison slave labor has always been a part of society's racist extended norm.

       Can you see me, can you feel me now, Miss?

Is it my traditional posture that gives doubt about my spinal pathway.
Is it uncomfortable to regard a black man as a superstitious being.
Symbolically throughout history, it seems.
You and your fictitious literature about our contributions to evolution.
Mentally and physically demoralizing us through your flow of pure bullshit
That comes from the outer limits.

       Can you see me, can you feel me now, Miss?

Always doing your balancing act for the masses of equality and righteousness.
While practicing genocide and mass destruction on an astronomical level.

       Can you see me, can you feel me now, Miss?

Let me enlighten you about my spinal vital forces.
My whole genetic makeup is strength. Your constant doubt benefits and awaken fibers
Deep within my subconscious center. Internal organs are directed to operate
In accordance to the black man's true design,
This only exists within the black man's melanin.

       Can you see me, can you feel me now, Miss?

Your words are nothing but moans and sentences to deaf ears. Tirades of whimpers,
Syntaxes locked within a tube of non-existence.

       Can you see me, can you feel me now, Miss?

It's redundant that you question the validity of my spinal cord, to find yours
One would have to search the archives of (Lost, but not to be found).

       Can you see me, can you feel me now, Miss?

Constraints of time are tightly woven around my neck,
As a constant reminder of yester-years events.

       Can you see me, can you feel me now, Miss?

I Want to Live

Reflections of warriors of the past keeps me focused,
Pushing to keep blackness forever in motion.

The trials and tribulations are daily struggles, while doing my utmost
To survive all this prison injustice.

      Can you see me, can you feel me now, Miss?

The white man is able to exploit, vent his deepest longings to abuse and annihilate
The black man and woman, that he himself has very little actual knowledge of,
But hella' power over of.

      Can you see me, can you feel me now, Miss?

In the back allies of his genetic makeup, there's a stored chemical imbalance,
That pushes him to act out his cowardice and barbaric homosexual deviant ways.

A predisposition which arrived upon his evolution.
Corruption, exploitation, genocide, bigotry. From the basic to the most perverse of forms.
Men who have no qualms or empathy surrounding their savagery and vicious acts
Towards mankind.

Manipulated through education has us blind inside.
The great plague of all times.
The driving force of turmoil and racism.

I hope you can see me,

At least you can feel me No? Huh, Miss?

Still
Haneef Walid

1555 Blackness born in the Americas.
Religion, ancestry, heritage & culture torn.
STILL BLACK LIVES MATTER!
Mentally, physically & emotionally whipped,
Just to build a New World as masta deemed fit.
STILL BLACK LIVES MATTER!
Strong wills broken & families torn apart.
Human beings sold as cattle down at local markets.
STILL BLACK LIVES MATTER!
If whipping posts could talk, they'd tell a tale of horrors.
Beaten backs for rebellious acts of men considered less than human.
STILL BLACK LIVES MATTER!
This lynching of a nation was just its incubation.
Because the seeds of these deeds sowed the woes of today's Black American sorrows.
STILL BLACK LIVES MATTER!
To where today my brother is my enemy,
& the mother of my child is my bitch.
Education & religion deemed suck shit.
Where nigga flows freely off every races' lips.
STILL BLACK LIVES MATTER!
Though we've suffered the torments of Job & Jonan,
Racial politics & liquor stores on every corner.
BLACK LIVES STILL MATTER!
Genetic genocide & drive - by homicides, we thrive because
BLACK LIVES STILL MATTER!
With minds that created art, infrastructure, medicine, & commodities,
Discoveries thought to be impossibilities, we thrive because
BLACK LIVES STILL MATTER!
Because without Black America, there's no America.
Land of the free built on the backs of the slave.
BLACK LIVES STILL MATTER!
For the people, By the people,
We are
Still

I Want to Live

Dedication
Antwan Carter

Glass shatters, bullets blast the world screams
Black lives matter!
Mothers cry as children die but what is society after
Gruesome acts caught on camera but justice still goes unnoticed
Surrounded by big clouds of distrust you wonder why we so hopeless
"I can't breathe" was the sound of a black man being choked to death!
Subsequently the whole world waited anxiously to see the Grand Jury's decision
An what we saw was partly shocking but deep down we knew what to expect
Take a closer look before words were spoken bullets greeted Tamir Rice
His sister manhandled as if she was a criminal
Come on, do they really value our life!???
Black lives matter, it's more like black lives don't matter in this day and age
Where blacks are viewed as dollars, check it, we still like slaves
Funny how we're more known as athletes, musicians and comics than anything else
Just yesterday I turned on the TV to see on the news
Chicago released a video from over a year
Where less than 60 seconds 16 shots we fired
How many stories do I have to tell for you to shed a tear?
Society we at war with a system that cannibalizes people based off the color of their skin
They say ignorance is bliss and racism no longer exists because of having a Black president
I crack a big smile instantly because I can see their effortless claims
Lady liberty! persuade Amerikkka to change its filthy ways
Before we burn this shit down in flames! . . .

Uncle Tom
Matt Shepard

I'm the last to play the race card,
But I can see the pain from slavery's scars,
The dimmed lights from civil rights,
I'm black, so I fight. Not the old fight but the new fight,
Where I empathize and justify a racist behavior,
Methodical, logical reasons, the words of a traitor,
I serve the people, but what does that mean?
I say that they're not racist, but what have I seen?
Maybe they are not and it's a cultural thing,
Repulsed by the sagging, cursing and flashy bling - bling,
DAMN! I just did it again, defending my master,
Searching for daddy's approval for a boy born a bastard,
DAMN! DAMN! It's just so hard to accept,
I've grown so much but this measures my depth,
I'm treated so good and I'm invited into their house,
Fed the same food so I refuse to curse them with my mouth,
DAMN! DAMN! DAMN! I help them maintain order . . . (smh),
"BLACK LIVES MATTER" and I say we killing each other,
Say my brother, I only want what's best for you,
We oppressed by the police, so why would we loot?
Get on your deem and do what you are supposed to do,
Pull your pants up, put your hands up so these cowards won't shoot,
They not gonna kill me 'cause I'm gone be where I'm supposed to be,
Not robbing a store, selling L. U. C. I.'s or ducked under a hoodie,
DAMN! DAMN! DAMN! . . . DAMN! I just did it again,
Why do I keep committing the same mistake?
I choose love while they strategize hate,
Killed for not understanding, how much more can I take?
OK . . . WAIT . . . I think that I got it,
YOU pulled YOUR weapon and YOU shot it,
Accept the decisions that you make, is what the master say,
DAMN! That's just a defense to live to see another day

To Black Men
Rodney "Peddiewack" Glaze

Black Man, Black Man, Peep This Out,
If we keep killing each other,
We will wipe ourselves out,
Open your eyes, and tell me what you don't see,
Fewer Black Man walkin' the streets,
Yeah! these prisons are full of Black Men like me,
3-strikes and you're out,
Designed for "You and Me,"
Got one strike,
For being born Black,
And it's hard to get a job,
Just because of that,
Day after day, same old shit,
Living expenses, got to pay the rent,
Can't break the Law,
But I dropped out of school,
"Black Man, Black Man"
Your loved ones need you,
And your kids do too,
"Black Man, Black Man,"
Hear Me out,
If Black lives matter,
Let's help each other out

I Object
Douglas/E'Vone Dawkins

Liberty restricted
With no respect

The black identity,
Under house arrest

Endangered
But labeled suspect

Law enforced,
Hatred unchecked

Sanctioned
By political elects,

Whom do they serve
Whom do they protect

Subordinates
And rednecks

Since the airing
Of shogun, no one
Has stopped to reflect

Inner city violence
Is a project

Ulterior motives,
We fail to detect

Landmines triggered
By colored steps,
Misguided
By community reps

Duplicity
Of the moral right,

I Want to Live

Absence of
The political left

Police armed
Despite failed psych tests
Whole communities
Sentenced to death
By maniacs
In bullet proof vests

Equal justice?
Don't hold your breath!

Black folks pawns
In genocide chess

Oppressive courts
Versus black flesh

D.A.'s dealing from
The bottom of the deck

Judge: "hang 'em high"
"I object!"

To internal affairs . . .
Gross neglect

To Remain Untitled
Jonathon Gordon

The cavemen left the caucus then
Livin' out their evil lives in godless sin
They mocked god by dividing him up and puttin' him in cloths n skin
The cavemen terrorized everyone from Afrikans in loincloths and huts
To Native Americans in teepees and moccasins
We try to get out of poverty but the KKK block us in
Tryin' to keep all Afrikan Americans jobless, then
Their only migration up outta poverty and the hood is the jailhouses
And prisons they lock us up in
Since their boats docked up in

The harbors of the Western Atlantic
Caucasians communities have been harboring extremists and fanatics
Frantic in carrying out their schematics and antics

So what what? — We're supposed to give thanks to the Pilgrims?
The Pilgrims who ROBBED the Natives raped women and killed them?
Even today the actions of the cavemen's descendants is still grim
With hatred filled to the brim -
Just look at Marcus Garvey and MLK and what they billed them
Then look at Malcolm X, what about Muhammad Ali, what they billed him

He was stripped of the right to practice his profession and lectured
He was publicly humiliated/disgraced by the AmeriKKKlan prefecture
For his right to be a conscientious objector
He didn't fight a White man's war and be a KKK protector
He said he ain't got no beef with Charlie

The cavemen want us to go overseas to kill or die so they can gather
Other people's riches and hoard it
While at home our own fights for freedom and citizenship
Are being aborted
Extremism/radicalism by Whites is government sponsored/supported
That's why Black/Brown & Muslim people get deported
But before they do — their cheap labor is exploited and extorted

I Want to Live

The U. S. of KKK wants stop Black/Brown/Muslim people's migrations
In order to keep AmeriKKKa a majority WHITE nation
And make a new KKKountry for people whose skin got darker pigments
It's called PRISON — no this isn't no figment
Of my imagination, and it ain't no conspiracy theory
These theories be no fanatical heresy it's a real conspiracy
That's carried out — every day — FEARLESSLY

And religiously/insidiously/ridiculously and conspicuously
It's warfare — mentally and physically
Under the pretense/guise/trickology of Christianity
In reality it's pure frickin' INSANITY
Backed up by right wings fanatics like Limbaugh, Combs, and Hannity

The cavemen confuse their acts of terrorism
With valor and heroism
In their narrow vision
They see themselves as great redeemers
Sent by God to save/eradicate AmeriKKKa from the Muslims and DREAMERS
They see Black men/women drivin' Benzes and Beemers

Or walking down the street with hoodies
Then it's "probable cause" to go on a witch-hunt for dope baggies,
Guns, and any little goodies

With "probable cause" they can now Stop-n-Frisk or Terry Stop
Boys/girls ask, "Mommy why did daddy get beat by them scary cops?"
Eyewitnesses record the incidents on iPhones & the videos go viral
Police wonder why disconnect with Afrikan Americans spirals & spirals
With accusations of racism & brutality, their eyes roll

Claimin' that racism in their department ain't prevalent
They go to the grave denying the fact it's still relevant or evident
He pretends that he's a heaven-sent

Afrikan Americans/Latinos/Asians/Natives is afraid to call the cops
Because they know it'll come back to hurt ya later
When the victims become suspects and perpetrators
And perpetrators get HURT BY TRAITORS!

Who betrayed their oath to uphold the law, protect and serve and

Uphold the constitution
With convolutions, and constant intrusions into legally
Protected territory
Now, here's a story

If your skin's peanut butter, ebony, or like a jaguar
It's justification for AmeriKKKA to keep your life in quagmires
The KKKaveman's mouth shoots out euphemisms/epithets like mag fires

While pridefully raising the AmeriKKKan/KKKonfederate flags higher
Giving all credit for technology/innovation/civilizing to their face
Taking all the glory — pretending to be holier than thou and chaste
They took history, distorted it, and Afrika's best parts
Were erased/monuments defaced

KKKaucasions refuse to accept their origins,
They don't want to acknowledge Afrika is in their deoxy ribonucleic acid
Their refusal to accept the TRUE progenitors is tacit
But they can never get past it, the facts are

They TOO originate from the Afrikan man/woman's loins and seed
And Afrika is in their genes/DNA when they bleed

I Want to Live

Not Worker, But Chattel
Ivan Kilgore

Whereas the positionality of the worker (whether a factory worker demanding a monetary wage, an immigrant, or a white woman demanding a social wage) gestures toward the reconfiguration of civil society, the positionality of the Black subject (whether a prison-slave or a prison-slave-in-waiting) gestures toward the misconfiguration of civil society. From the coherence of civil society, the Black subject beckons with the incoherence of civil war, a war that reclaims Blackness not as a positive value, but as a politically enabling site, to quote Fanon, of "absolute dereliction." It is a "scandal" that rends civil society asunder. Civil war, then, becomes the unthought, but never for-gotten, understudy of hegemony. It is a Black specter waiting in the wings, an endless antagonism that cannot be satisfied (via reform or reparation), but must nonetheless be pursued to the death.

—**Frank B. Wilderson III**. "The Prison Slave as Hegemony's (Silent) Scandal," *Social Justice*. Vol. 30, No. 2 (2003): 26.

One of the most overlooked contradictions that imprisoned abolitionists face today is not merely the issue of our resistance meeting a master's repression, nor is it a matter of fending off the Democratic Party's attempt to co-opt—to steal and covertly misdirect—our efforts into the legal machine of Civil Rights reform. What we prison slaves and millions of other "prison-slaves-in-waiting" have yet to comprehend is the extent to which an internal ideological struggle must be waged among ourselves, within a segregated prison population, as well as in our neighborhoods and communities, if we are ever to realize our potential as revolutionary class.

What I convey in the following essay is a particular lesson regarding what Hortense J. Spillers calls "the intramural" (Hortense J. Spillers, *Mama's Baby, Papa's Maybe: An American Grammar Book*, Diacritics 1987) derived from my experience organizing side-by-side with fellow U.S. prison slaves. It is a story about the white supremacist state's use of deprivation, terror, seduction, and organized treachery as tactics to maintain compliance and 'order' among the imprisoned masses. It is a story of the past and an analysis of the present, to clarify the trajectory for our struggle moving forward—without promise, without confirmation of an eventual justice, drawing only upon our collective abolitionist faith. In what follows, I argue that a Black abolitionist politics—a set of beliefs and practices formed in opposition to the white supremacist state; struggles for life and death initiated by and for those inhabiting the social position of chattel property—must both be definitively against "work" and against defining ourselves as "workers." As a number of Black Studies scholars write, there are fundamental differences be-tween the political category of the "worker" and that of the "slave."

Rendered civilly dead by U.S. law, I am to the State as the slave was to the plantation Master. The same relation of coercive racist violence applies: my Black body is always vulnerable, open to an enveloping State terror. As property of the State, I exist in direct confrontation with the punitive core of capitalist relations of force. Every movement I make carries with it the possibility of authority's lash. I am the bodily raw material that gives the prison industrial complex purpose and social meaning. Beyond recognizing the structure of violence that I inhabit; it should also be noted how the very act of naming myself—a slave held captive by the State—as "worker" enables various tactics of seduction which operate to displace the gravity of the situation. Because job assignments are seen as a relative privilege behind these walls, we are lured into conformity and compliance to work, often merely out of a need to survive. While I discuss this latter dilemma for the majority of this essay, I would first like to begin by unpacking the former, clarifying the structural position of the (prison) slave.

I.

There are two essential dilemmas that prisoners face when organizing as the worker-on-strike instead of the slave-in-revolt. One is that a prison strike must be organized differently, its operations conducted differently, and requires a level of active solidarity (from others not in our position, non-imprisoned people) far greater than any other united workplace action. Many on the outside need to take up more of the risk. For example, there are numerous ways that free-world people can participate in a prison strike that does not mistake symbolic action for direct, disruptive tactics. We need mass civil disobedience, not more civic performance. If our goal is to clog the arteries of the prison regime from within, it might be more effective to choose methods that interrupt the prison's reproduction from without. While we are staging sit-ins, boycotts, stoppages, and refusing trays inside, free-world activists could occupy the offices of a Department of Corrections, stage protests at a prison warden's private house, or stage sit-ins in the buildings of government institutions and corporations that benefit from the smooth functioning of the prison-crat's political-industrial machine. As an outside comrade once pointed out, "phone zaps" are effective in certain historical situations, but disrupting this fascist regime requires a whole lot more.

As Frank B. Wilderson III argues, the worker is exploited at best, yet only shot, brutalized, or imprisoned because they engage in sabotage or forceful strike. The slave however is rendered the object of gratuitous violence as a perpetual structural constant. By missing this point and defining ourselves as imprisoned "workers," we open ourselves up to the public's misrecognition of the levels of risk involved with organizing on the inside. The universalist category of the worker also fails to grasp the centrality of our captivity to the making of U.S. society's sense of (racial) freedom and (white) civilizational ascendancy over the wretched of the earth. This, in fact, brings me to my second point, a thing much more complex to explain. That is, the fact that our enslavement by the State holds a culturally specific purpose for the society that appears driven to physically disappear us.

I Want to Live

In the antebellum South, plantation slavery was not only an institution for the production of material goods at a cheap cost for the ruling class. Slavery established the very structure through which white freedom was, and is, made legible. The machinery of slavery was foundational to the non-slave's experience of freedom at a psycho-social level. In fact, there would be no need to use the word "freedom" at all had there not first been the creation of a structural position called the Slave. It has always been white freedom and life produced in opposition to Black unfreedom and death. State power is not only repressive but productive of social relations. It creates traps that lure us into complicity and participation whether it is for our own benefit or not. We need to understand work in prisons as such, and promote an abolitionist politic that is profoundly anti-work. We can't see the struggle as merely a fight for better wages, because the majority of us don't have wages at all. We have to abolish the apparatus that cages us, separates us from our families, and disappears us from our communities. We need a movement that thinks not only in terms of labor/economics, but a movement that challenges the carceral foundations of the white supremacist state.

Often, when I tell fellow prisoners of my reluctance to work in one of the many prison factories or so-called "job assignments," I am looked upon as if I have said something foolish. They always defer to the question of "Why?" As if being exploited for pennies on the dollar or no wage at all for our labor is an acceptable situation. In answering their question, I explain to them my experience in the Seminole County Jail in Wewoka, Oklahoma. For twenty-three months, I was trapped in that Barney Fife of a hellhole, fighting for my life on a capital murder charge. It had no commissary. No TV or radio. No outside cell activity. No library. Nothing. We were housed six to a cell, and all we had were our bunks, a few card games, and what few books we could get our hands on. Lunch was reheated for dinner and, needless to say, the food was terrible. So terrible that almost twenty-five years later I still can taste that stale Thursday morning breakfast. It was degrading; an army ration of dehydrated ham and egg. Mixed with a little hot water it swelled up like dry dog shit on a rainy summer day. After flushing it down the toilet for about six months I finally relented. When you lose thirty pounds from starvation you begin to acquire a taste for this sort of shit. Of course, the trustees (i.e., slaves with "work privileges") were allowed to watch TV, listen to radio, and to use the soda machine upstairs in the courthouse. Every now and then, the jailor would also allow one of them to go across the street to the Dollar General to purchase candy, underwear, deodorant, or some other miscellaneous item that seemed to make life in that shit-hole that much more tolerable. (In case you're wondering, the only clothing the jail provided were the oversized, bright orange jumpsuits; no coats, underwear, etc.). They also were allowed a hug and kiss from their visitors and, on the weekends, they worked maintenance on the courtyard. As for the rest of us, we were allowed nothing. No commissary, no TV, no outside cell activity. Nothing. Old cornbread, wrapped in some toilet paper wrapper, was the only the thing we had to eat that kept our stomachs from growling at night. Man, how I wished to be a "trustee" during those days. The "perks" alone made it to where nobody in that situation, including myself, cared that we were in fact being paid nothing for our labor.

For twenty-three months, I was forced to live under the foregoing conditions, wanting nothing besides freedom, and willing to slave just to get a small taste of it. Yet because I was charged with a M1 (i.e., 1st-degreee-murder-charge) and would later face a death penalty trial, there would be no listening to country music or enjoying the sliver of mobility awarded to a trustee. Looking back on that situation today, I cannot help but think of how un-freedom and "gut" starvation conditioned me. I internalized so much stress, fear, and anger that it tempered my spirit. I failed to even realize how profoundly it suspended my reluctance to work in a carceral setting. Essentially, I was disciplined to withstand the taunting effects of my incarceration which prompt so many of us slaves to relent to the illusive "perks" associated with prison labor and a life of hardscrabble.

Eventually, I was able to place those so-called perks in their proper perspective: They were but a distraction, misplaced values and desires I had yet to conquer; things that I had been manipulated to hold in esteem that, with exception of food and exercise, were not necessarily needed to sustain life. They were but a carrot-on-a-stick, an inducement used to exercise power over my being by misleading me to believe they were privileges; yet, because I could not value a privilege I did not have, or be made content by it, the power my captors sought to exercise over me was ineffective. Little did I realize at the time how this enabled me to see my situation for what it truly was—a grave injustice—and respond accordingly. Instead of submitting to the distraction and attempting to ameliorate the harsh conditions of my incarceration with an elusive perk, I learned how to use those conditions as a source of motivation to fight for my freedom and just treatment.

In short, I TURNED UP! Food trays were thrown at the jailors and trustees. Mattresses burned. The entire jail flooded, and the power short-circuited. I fired attorneys left and right, and began the processes of learning how to represent myself in court. Ultimately, I won and was back on the streets in 36 months. In time, I was to discover my experience in Oklahoma was not typical compared with most county jails and prison systems created by this settler colonial nation. To put it mildly, the Seminole County Jail was a relic of the Old South, where doing time was and still is, in many aspects, harsh and unbearable. Years later, when I was committed to the California Department of Corrections and Rehabilitation (CDCR), one of the first of many cellies I was to have over the years called himself schooling me on the hustle and perks of prison work assignments. The perks, he explained, ranged from something as simple as stealing extra food from the kitchen, to manipulating staff for sex and other "contraband." Indeed, the inducement to work seemed to have its advantages.

However, as he explained all of this, I could not help but think that while he meant no harm with his advice, he was thinking ass-backwards. At this point, he had done almost twenty calendar years. And what he was kickin' to me was hustling to be content with his life in prison and being "penitentiary rich." As time passed and we became better aquatinted with one another, I eventually pointed out to him that neither the "perks" or anything he had hustled for in almost 20 years of being incarcerated has purchased his freedom, or created any kind of financial stability either inside or outside these walls. I explained that hustling in prison, more so than hustling on the bricks, is short-lived. It's corner hustling at its worst, dealing with shifty-ass scavengers, opportunists and scalawags—REAL LIFE DOPE FIEND SHIT! Where snitching is at an all-time high and it's a hit-and-miss inconsistent game where the hustlers, often more than not, wind up in the "hole" with more time, restrictions, and most defeating, giving their hustle stacks back to the canteen or their own habits.

Despite having explained all this, none of it seemed to register with him or countless other prisoners who, because of a lack of productive opportunities, confidence, knowledge, discipline, and plausibility of instant gratification, disregard the odds and relent to the bullshit. In time, I observed that it wasn't even about the hustle and perks for most prisoners. Many were simply looking for an escape from the daily monotony of an otherwise drab existence. Prisons, we know, are idle and mundane places. They are isolating. And the majority of us do not have the fortune of frequent, or any, interaction with the outside world. Therefore, to be able to get out of the cell to work—especially in a maximum-security setting—and to be able to fraternize with other inmates or staff—especially those staff who are comfortable sharing their life experiences, which many prisoners have yet to have, if ever they will—is vicariously and psychologically rewarding in and of itself.

Having observed the foregoing, it became abundantly clear that while the majority of us are conscious of the fact that our labor is being exploited, the value we have come to place on a work assignment has been manipulated by the structural environment created by prison officials. To this end, we know prisons are purposefully designed to be cruel and unusual places. And despite countless court rulings ameliorating the abuse we frequently encounter at the hands of prison administrators, the intent remains to maintain oppressive conditions that, in effect, aim to keep us impoverished, dependent and, thus, powerless. Consequently, this has given life to the culture that we subscribe to where, for example, pushing a broom on the tier for 20 years with little to no compensation is accepted as a norm so long as we may entertain the illusion of a "come up."

II.

"Neither slavery nor involuntary servitude, except as a punishment for crime whereof the party shall have been duly convicted, shall exist within the United States, or any place subject to their jurisdiction." —13th Amendment of the United States Constitution

"Prison slavery" over the past decade has gained traction as a keyword in activist vocabularies and progressive popular culture. Some people use the term to describe the conditions of cheap or literal indentured labor that I discuss above. Yet over time, it has taken on a new and more adequate meaning referring to the generalized condition of a prisoner's social death. Slavery in this theoretical context is the legally-sanctioned and state-condoned project of containing and disappearing certain targeted and criminalized populations—the social condition that animates the machinery of the U.S. Prison-Industrial Complex; a white supremacist regime with its own separate drives that exceed the demands of wealth accumulation. Of course, punishment has been industrialized as a means to manage various (criminalized) surplus populations, those deemed unqualified or ineligible for even the most exploitative of waged occupation. Yet at its core modern prison slavery is also predicated on a distinctly white supremacist logic of extermination (for more on the concept of "logic of extermination," see: Dylan Rodriguez. *Forced Passages: Imprisoned Radical Intellectuals in the U.S. Prison Regime.* Minneapolis: University of Minnesota Press, 2006).

The Thirteenth Amendment, according to this argument, is a legal technology that has anchored U.S. geopolitical power in a foundation of Black genocide. This mass of white supremacist violence is not confined only to the physical site of the prison/jail itself, but is also a basis for the white settler's entire conception of himself as "free," as the proper subject of "rights," as the allegedly peaceful guardian a "democratic" social order. It is the removal of criminalized populations from white civil space that enables the U.S. settler to think they are free. The structural violence of prison slavery is thus modeled on the master-over-slave relation, yet in the present era it has been transfigured into the state-over-convict relation. The latter figure is effectively eviscerated of all "rights" under law and placed in a position of government-imposed civil/social death.

In 2014, Free Alabama Movement co-founders Melvin Ray, Kinetic Justice, and I were discussing the prospect of kicking off a "Free California Movement" in which California prisoners would join the international movement to abolish prison slavery. My initial response was, "It'll never work in Cali." Why? To be clear, in no way was my response a reflection of my own disposition, but rather it was a reflection of the many conversations I have had on the subject over the years with fellow prisoners. Time and time again, what they say is, "Man . . . I ain't got not outside support. I can't risk losing my job. That $10, $50 and, in some cases $200 pay number, counts!'" or it's "I'm trying to 'come up'!" And I can't forget the chow hall workers. They like to eat! It's that simple. (And that's not to mention how all the recent changes in law that now provide earned time credits and parole consideration have impacted them in such a way that "protesting" anything is the last thing they're concerned about). For them the inducement to work is simply too strong. Then, of course, there are those who honestly believe they owe a debt to society. Therefore, they see nothing wrong with their enslavement.

All this Melvin and Kinetic Justice couldn't believe. They were simply astonished and under the impression that there would be a strong resistance to injustice within California's prison population, on account of George Jackson's legacy and the 2011/2013 hunger strikes in which a reported 30,000 prisoners protested the renegade administrative process that landed countless people in the SHU indefinitely. To my dismay, I had to explain to them that the hunger strikes were a gradualist reform movement, not a militant abolitionist movement; that they had nothing to do with abolishing prison slavery or genocide more generally; that the majority of prisoners in California would view a general strike as counter-productive to their own selfish reasons for working in a prison setting, and like prisoners any- where many simply lacked the necessary vision, discipline, knowledge, and willingness to sacrifice those crumbs for the bigger picture.

Having said that, I've noticed a slight change of disposition amongst many prisoners in California. Before and during the hunger strikes, many were doubtful, if not pessimistic, as to our ability to bring about change and abolish many of the oppressive and inhumane aspects of prison. However, after the hunger strikes lead to the 2015 settlement in "Ashker v. Brown," which supposedly abolished indefinite SHU terms, the conversation on the yard has been somewhat optimistic. That said, the most significant result of the hunger strikes was not forcing CDCR to reform its bogus gang validation process and indeterminate SHU scheme, rather it was the cultivation of faith that we as prisoners—as a collective and enslaved political body—have the power to dismantle the oppressive and inhumane circumstances we find ourselves in. In essence, the hunger strikes exemplified what abolitionist Ruthie Gilmore describes as the mobilization of the forms of dual power already latent in colonized and oppressed communities; the disruptive potential of organizing ourselves as rebel slaves. She explains:

> Power is not a thing but rather a capacity composed of active and changing relationships enabling a person, group, or institution to compel others to do things they would not do on their own (such as be happy, or pay taxes, or go to war). Ordinarily, activists focus on taking power, as though the entire political setup were really a matter of 'it' (structure) versus 'us' (agency). But if the structure-agency opposition isn't actually how things really work, then perhaps politics is more complicated, and therefore open to more hopeful action. People can and do make power through, for example, developing capacities in organizations. But that's not enough, because all an individual organization can do on its own is tweak Armageddon. When the capacities resulting from purposeful action are combined toward ends greater than mission statements or other provisional limits, powerful alignments begin to shake the ground. In other words, movement happens.
>
> – Ruth Wilson Gilmore. *Golden Gulags: Prisons, Surplus, Crisis, and Opposition in Globalizing California.* Berkeley: University of California Press, 2007.

As emblematic as the hunger strikes were in demonstrating how counter-state forms of power are fortified, which Gilmore argues succinctly in the above passage, we still have our work cut out for us. The entire structure of prison slavery/genocide must be challenged as a whole. I believe it is important that we acknowledge the policing and imprisonment regime as the central target we rally around and develop the capacities of "power" that reside—dormant, always—within our communities. Just as it took slaves refusing trays, street protestors, progressive lawyers, university workers, and many others to build the 2011/13 resistance and provide documented evidence that long term solitary confinement is psychologically damaging and "cruel and unusual punishment," so too will the same effort be required to demonstrate that prison slavery in fact is programmatic, low-intensity Black genocide more generally.

Notably, the recent 2016 and 2018 nationwide prison strikes show promise. But we need more. We need to build a mass movement that wages an offensive for genocide abolition. What is needed is not merely slavery abolition, but the abolition of the prison as a lethal mechanism of social death. We must resist the seductions of work in an environment of forced isolation and (the always-present-potential for) extermination. In turn, we must not misconstrue our status as mere exploited workers, or model our operations on the lessons of striking wage workers. The position of the (prison) slave is a structural juncture of improvised unity with which we can all rally behind, whether locked in the gulag already, or as peoples struggling together on the outside to avoid/defend-against/abolish the possibility of capture. There is a power that we can utilize, a power that can be unleashed in the domino effect of the revolting slave. This is how Black political consciousness is formed—from the everyday to the extraordinary, in the anti-dialectic between master and slave, we continue to build the grounds upon which the former's disintegration becomes imperative. The chattel convict is thus from the moment of arrest positioned in such a way as to develop Black politics, as imprisoned people are all subjected to the gratuitous terror of the state. We are not workers for the most part. We are enslaved. Captive. Captured. Property of the U.S. nation state. The raw materials disappeared to give shape to white democracy's freedom. Free world abolitionists will you join in the dance with social death? (Frank Wilderson III. *Red, White and Black: Cinema and the Structure of U.S. Antagonisms*. Durham: Duke University Press, 2010.)

Black Lives Matter on Both Sides of the Fence
**Sitawa Nantambu Jamaa, James "Baridi" Williamson,
Yusuf Bey IV, and Ivan Kilgore**

> Slavery has been fruitful in giving itself names. It
> has been called "the Peculiar Institution", "the
> Social System", and "the Impediment" . . . It has
> been called by a great many names, and it
> will call itself by yet another name,
> and you and I and all of us had
> better wait and see what new
> form this old snake will
> come forth next . . .
>
> —Frederick Douglass, May 9, 1855

Have you ever read or heard about a click of rogue California correctional officers dubbed the "Green Wall?" What about the Oakland Police Department's "Riders?" Or the "Rampart Division" of tine LAPD? How about those "Gladiator Fights" orchestrated by prison officials at the California State Prison, Corcoran, which resulted in 31 prisoners killed by police bullets? Certainly, you heard about the white police officer in OKC who was recently sentenced to 266 years for raping black women? Or the 21 or better officers at the LA County jail who were recently sentenced to federal prison? And who could forget Rodney King or what racist pigs did with fire hoses during the 1960s? It wasn't that long ago.

Then there are the countless suspicious suicides and prisoner assassinations that have been rumored to have been setup by prison and jailhouse officials. And to think, for most of white America, this is simply a figment of the imagination. Yet it is a reality visited upon someone in this country every day! Sandra Bland and Hugo "Yogi Bear" Pinnell experienced it! Michael Brown experienced it too! So too Oscar Grant, Eric Garner, Tapir Rice, and sadly, countless others to come. That said, it's imperative that we do not attempt, with Black Lives Matter, to separate police terrorism on either side of the fence. For the streets ain't the only place law enforcement needs body cameras! Even more, it's imperative that we do not attempt a discourse on police terrorism without connecting it to judicial terrorism or judicial terrorism to penal, legislative or economic terrorism. For they are all of the same organism; a pathogen: capitalism, which strictly adheres to an age-old philosophy that deems the punishment justifiable (i.e., the incarceration, brutalization and, if necessary, the murder) of the innocent so as to maintain the "order" (i.e., the socio-economic and political arrangement) which fostered white supremacy.

Needless to say, it is a philosophy that gave way to a culture of racism, lawlessness and terrorism that very much remains at the heart of law enforcement in America to this day. And like most of that which came of Europe to the Americas, it was derived from the most corrupt, narcissistic, and lustful thoughts of its revered scholars: Hobbes (1533-1679), Locke (1632-1704), Montesquieu (1689-1755), Rousseau (1712-73), Blackstone (1723-80), Beccaria (1738-1794), and others who, during the so-called Enlightenment era, rationalized, for lack of better term, that Native Americans and Afrikans were but simple creatures of vice, and prone to acts of savagery—chattel, who lacked the moral capacity to determine what was just or cruel. In essence, the theory also applied to women, poor whites, and the diseased of Europe, and thus became the basis for colonial ideology.

This philosophy, this ideology of colonial imperialism, was recorded during the course of history as it spread throughout the Americas like a wild grass fire. Consequently, the Native bloodline and culture would suffer near extermination. Countless Creole and Latino ethnic groups bore the rape that came out of it. From Afrika to Europe, across the Caribbean Sea to the shores of the antebellum South, it would spread ivory Afrikan bones across the floor of the Atlantic Ocean. In the Old South, it would form the "Peculiar Institution" Frederick Douglass foresaw as the "old snake" shed its skin and took shape in the nation's system of criminal justice. The 13th Amendment to the U.S. Constitution would give it vigor, proclaiming slavery the appropriate punishment for crime. And so, it was written, with this legislative enactment, the "philosophy" became the foundation upon which a racist system of government policies and laws would spring forth to form the image of who and what would be criminalized. The purported "Founders" of "AmeriKKKa" had indeed studied their scholars well.

Rousseau had instructed the law was but "an invention of the strong to chain and rule the weak." And Montesquieu's Spirit of the Laws provided them justification to enslave Afrikans:

> . . . Since the peoples of Europe have exterminated those of America, they have had to enslave those of Africa in order to use them to clear and cultivate such a vast expanse of land.
>
> Sugar would be too expensive if it weren't harvested by slaves.
>
> Those in question are black from the tip of their toes to the top of their heads; and their noses so flattened that it is almost impossible to feel sorry for them.
>
> It is inconceivable that God, who is a very wise being, could have placed a soul, especially a good soul, in an all-black body . . .
>
> One proof of the fact that Negroes don't have any common sense is that they get more excited about a string of glass beads than about gold, which, in civilized countries, is so dearly prized.
>
> It is impossible that these people are men; because if we thought of them as men, one would begin to think that we ourselves are not Christians.

Henceforth, were white AmeriKKKa pillaged and murdered, the law would provide a banner of protection. And so, it was again written, their "collective conscience" was distorted with B.S. philosophy that allowed for their atrocities to be interpreted not as crimes against humanity, but rather, acts of patriotism "lawfully" wielded against chattel, savages and criminals. This is the genius of the law as practiced by Europe and white AmeriKKKa. It is the "power" to which Locke philosophized: "Great robbers punish little ones to keep them in their obedience; but the great ones are rewarded with laurels and triumphs, because they are too big for the weak hands of justice in this world, and have the power in their own possession which should punish offenders."

Another device of Europe with a long history beginning in 1657, under the corrupt regime of King Louis XIV, and considered by many a symbol of "foreign oppression" was the former slave catchers (and Ku Klux Klan, for that much) who were now the "police." (Note: The first attempts at police reform in Europe would not occur until 1829, when British statesman Sir Robert Peel formed what has been cited as the first full-time, professional and centrally organized police force—the London Metropolitan Police). Strapped with the task of upholding the "law," AmeriKKKan police in the South, very much like King Louis's, would serve an economic and social duty in service of the state, which largely overreached simple law enforcement activities.

According to Sultan Latif, author of *Slavery: The African American Psychic Trauma*, the first police departments "were established [in the South] post-civil war, when the abolition of slavery and the development of industrialization meant that there were massive laboring populations [of ex-slaves] that could no longer be disciplined by the slave-owner or individual task-master, but had to be supervised, as an industrial army, by a well-armed institutionalized force." In this regard, the police would become the force — as well as an extension of — organized crime, driving industrialization as the political machine in the South, quickly going to work to preserve white privilege.

Under the assumption the former slaves would not work unless compelled to do so, Black Codes were enacted. An offshoot of Slave Codes, they were specifically designed with the intent to control, restrict, and inhibit the ex-slave's movement and behavior. Moreover, Black Codes defined crime for all purposes and intent of re-enslaving the freedmen and women, and thus bestowed upon the police the "authority of the law" to arrest and charge, for example, unemployed Afrikans with "vagrancy," a crime pursuant to §§ of the Code. This, of course, created the presumption of wrongdoing which then led to a sham trial, and a fine the accused could not pay. Consequently, many Afrikans were banished to prison labor camps where their labor was then sold under the "Convict Leasing System" to local industry owners, such as steel and coal titan Andrew Carnegie, who, along with countless others, profited on the hundreds-of-millions, if not billions, of dollars from a labor pool of scarred backs and broken souls.

Considering the South's long and dependent history on slavery, and the bustling industries that began to take shape prior to and after the Civil War, the labor that came of these camps, needless to say, was in great demand. Despite legislative attempts to criminalize exploiting black lives for the purposes of its labor, the demand for prison labor far exceeded legislative production. Thus, white AmeriKKKa resorted back to the ways of their not-so-distant ancestors and began again to kidnap Afrikans to sell into this new form of slavery. However, the kidnappers were the police, local sheriffs and constables who levied fabricated charges and debts at Afrikans (to make their "quotas") to supply the demand.

In a 2008 interview, Douglas A. Blackmon, author of *Slavery by Another Name: The Re-Enslavement of Black Americans from the Civil War to World War II*, elaborated on the grandiosity of this racket:

> . . . it was everywhere in the South. These forced labor camps were all over the place. The records that still survive, buried in courthouses all over the South, make it abundantly clear that thousands and thousands of African Americans were arrested on completely specious claims, made up stuff, and then, purely because of this economic need [for prison labor] and the ability of sheriffs and constables and others to make money off arresting them, and that providing them to these commercial enterprises, and being paid for that.

As if the manner to which Afrikans had found themselves trapped and banished to these camps weren't enough, they were then charged for the cost of their confinement (e.g., food, clothes, etc.) and thus acquired debit on top of debit, which could never be paid. Consequently, many were condemned to die in bondage with this the arrangement. Others would also suffer from the tragedy that came of cruel and unusual prison conditions, which often, because of mining disasters, illness, hypothermia, or worse, a severe lashing, resulted in thousands of fatalities. (Note: The punishment associated with slavery was also incorporated into the penal system. The U.S. Supreme Court upheld prisoner whippings until 1958. See Jackson v. Bishop, 40A F.2d 571, 573.)

By the mid-1920s, the scale of this racket had reached its height and began to unravel as mounting complaints regarding the ruinous and unfair competition of prison labor from competing industry owners began to flood the U.S. Attorney General's Office. Again, the snake would shed its skin as a result of several legislative enactments (i.e., the Hawes-Cooper Act 1929); Ashurst-Summers Act (1935), a.k.a. 18 U.S.C. §1761(a); and the Walsh-Healey Act (1938)), which "temporarily" put a halt on the convict leasing system and the manufacture of prisoner-made products for public or private sale and distribution. In 1979, however, private interests again successfully lobbied for an amendment to 13 U.S.C. §1761, which set the grinders back in motion.

Without question, "[c]onvict leasing," as noted by Dan Berger, author of *Captive Nation*, "was the premiere element that made the Southern legal apparatus—from the police to the courthouse and the prison—a formidable foundation of the Jim Crow South." Notably, by the end of the Reconstruction Era (1857-77), all southern states had gone back and passed laws that weren't called Black Codes, but essentially aimed to subjugate

Afrikans as a second-class, inferior race. These laws would affectionately become known as "Jim Crow Laws."

With the emergence of Jim Crow, the question of race in AmeriKKKa sprung to the forefront of debate on both sides of the political spectrum. For white AmeriKKKans, it promised relief from the pervasive "Negro Problem," which threatened to assimilate into mainstream white society if not segregated (a form of confinement/containment). For Afrikans, it was an abomination, an impediment, to say the least, to social, political and economic progress. Unsurprisingly, the nation's high court weighed in to provide legal support to validate segregation as a social norm. The infamous (Dred) Scott v. Stanford (1857), Plessy v. Ferguson (1896), and William v. State of Mississippi (1393), respectfully, proclaimed among other controversies, Afrikans, "were unfit to associate with the white race and so far, inferior, that they have no rights which the white man was bound to respect." Moreover, these cases set forth in theory and practice the concept of "separate but equal," and lynch-mob trials by all white juries. Notably, the decisions made in these cases were premised on Darwin's (1809-82) theories of evolution, yet another device of Europe, which deemed Afrikans and other people of color biologically and intellectually inferior to whites.

Again, the police would be summoned to serve their social and economic duty in service of the state. According to Berger:

> American confinement [i.e., segregation] was upheld by the police as well as the prison. As in the South, the police in the North and West constituted a frontline battleground over white supremacy. Whereas the southern legal apparatus dictated segregation across social and political arenas, the formal equality of the North was undermined by pervasive racialized poverty that the police, as an institution, enforced at every step. Through violence and ritual humiliation, police departments enforced spatial boundaries of segregation and "vice" at the street level . . . [and therefore] became a common but foreign presence in the life of black urban denizens . . . [and consequently] led to greater institutionalization of black women and men in reformatories, jails and prisons. Indeed, the police and the judge joined the social worker as embodiments of the ways the American state regulated black lives . . .

Ghettos, yet another device of Europe that was used to isolate and exterminate Jews, were subsequently created as mass populations of Afrikans and other people of color were corralled into underdeveloped communities segregated by law, by violence and discriminatory government and private housing practices. Sundown Towns were created, which up until the late 1980s, allowed for lily-white towns and communities across AmeriKKKa to enforce written and unwritten ordinances that forbid people of color from taking residence in, or being within, city limits after dark. "NIGGER DON'T LET THE

SUN; GO DOWN BEFORE LEAVING TOWN" or "NO NIGGERS OR MEXICANS ALLOWED AFTER DARK" were posted on the outskirts of these towns, and enforced by lynching, torching of homes and entire communities, and brutal beatings by the police.

To be brief with this history is unkind, yet if there ever was a word, of all words in the English language, that accurately describes the social and economic turmoil that was to come of this arrangement, that word undoubtably would be "terrorism." Particularly, "economic terrorism" which, for purposes of this essay, we define as structural conditions shaped by institutional forces set on destroying the socio-economic and political development of a particular people. As history etched itself towards the 1960s, Afrikans would see the economic fabric of their communities torched in the wake of white supremacy. In 1921, Black Wall Street (Tulsa, OK) would be burned to the ground. In the decades to come, so too, would a number of other Afrikan communities across AmeriKKKa. The carnage would stack high well into the 1940s and beyond. With the passage of the 1949 Federal Housing Act, more than 400,000 homes in Afrikan communities across AmeriKKKa were destroyed under the guise of urban renewal.

By 1952, the Veteran's Administration and the FHA had financed more than $120 billion dollars in new housing, with less than 2% going to non-white families, and they built roughly 10,000 low-rent, segregated public housing units (a.k.a. "Projects"). (Note: In time, the projects would be "fenced up, their perimeter[s] placed under beefed-up security patrols and authoritarian controls, including identification card checks, signing in, electronic monitoring, police infiltration, random searches, curfews, and resident counts...." (Wacquant, 2002)). Urban renewal quickly came to symbolize "Negro Removal," as housing segregation grew into a nexus of racial inequality on all fronts, from employment opportunities to education. History foretold a rebellion would be forth going. Afrikans had fought the kidnappers who invaded the Motherland. We had fought and died on the ships. We rebelled on the plantations. We rebelled against Jim Crow. And so too the Natives fought the butchers of their lands. And so came an era, just as we fought side-by-side during the First and Second Seminole Wars (1812-42), we would fight together during the Civil Rights, Black Liberation, Puerto Rican Independence, AIM, anti-war, and student protest movements of the 1960s and '70s.

It goes without saying we were militant, organized and, at times, lethal — not to mention extremely outspoken when it came to matters of race and class oppression. The gun would become our symbol of liberation as we quickly came to grips with a truth echoed in the rhetoric of Black Panther Alprentice "Bunchy" Carter:

> ... Weapons of words won't deal with the Man. I think history has taught us that. The Man is a beast, and he's armed against us. The only thing that will deal with the Man is the gun, and men willing to use the gun.

And so, we stood as a collective, as violent encounters with local law enforcement erupted around the nation. Both militant and Police blood alike would fill the gutters of the barrios, ghettos and reservations, as the fear of us aggrandizing our "Nation," struck at the heart of the "powers-that-be." In response, COINTELPRO, an FBI subdivision headed by J. Edgar Hoover—was launched to disrupt, misdirect, and otherwise "neutralize" the leadership of these movements. Black Panther Ericka Huggins would tell of the devastation that came of this police force as in the following:

> [This] left many people dead, my husband John Huggins and Alprentice Carter another. The [COINTELPRO] did not start with the [Black Panther Party]; it began to do its heinous dirty work with people like [Dr. Martin Luther' King, Jr.] and the Civil Rights Movement at all levels. Its intention was, as they said, to wipe out the [Black Panther Party] by 1969... Looking back at it, taxpayers are appalled at what their money went to: setting up situations where, for instance, John Huggins and Alprentice Carter could be killed at UCLA... The FBI setup the circumstances for that; then the print media said it was Black-on-Black crime. But the FBI was a teacher for us. We learned to look at how insidious and subtle the work of a huge bureaucracy is and how fatal it could be for a small group of people who rebel against the status quo. So, the FBI harmed, tortured, harassed and set up the circumstances to kill directly or indirectly many, many, people in the [Black Panther Party]... Hoover urged his special agents to "prevent the coalition of militant black nationalists' groups... and leaders from gaining respectability... Prevent the rise of a black messiah who would unify and electrify the militant Black Nationalist Movement.

Consequently, Malcolm X, Dr. Martin Luther King, Jr., Bobby Hutton, Jonathan and George Jackson, Fred Hampton, and many other political leaders would be assassinated. Mumia Abu-Jamal, Suniate Acoli, Mondo we Lanna, Leonard Pelteir, Imam Jamil Al-Amin, and Mutulu Shakar were amongst a number of political activists subjected to "sham" trials and convictions which condemned many to either a life sentence in prison or the death house. Indeed, the devastation caused by COINTELPRO would be far-reaching.

By the early 1970s the assassination and incarceration of our political leaders had created a climate of loss and chaos that in the years and decades to come, was ripe for the growth of an urban gang element. Feelings of disempowerment again began to boil over from a lack of political resistance. This in turn, would ignite the self-hatred that had been festering in our communities for centuries. Suddenly, the spirit of resistance we had developed, which was grounded in the oppositional belief that white power was limited, that it could be challenged and transformed, went from employing violence as a countermeasure, to oppression, to inner-community violence aimed to oppress. To this end, Amos Wilson, author of *Black-on-Black Violence: The Psychodynamics of Black Self-Annihilation in Service of White Domination*, would inform us: "The violently oppressed react violently to their oppression. When their reactionary violence, their retaliatory or destructive violence, cannot be effectively directed at their oppressors or effectively applied to their self-liberation, it then will be directed at and applied destructively to themselves [. . .]."

No words better express the point in context as those of the late Stanley "Tookie" Williams, author of *Blue Rage, Black Redemption*:

> My rage was nourished by the hate I saw and felt from mainstream society and white people, a hate based on my black skin and my historical place at the nadir of America's social caste. I was filled with hate for injustice. Yet my reaction to the hate was violence directed only towards blacks.
>
> . . . I forged through much of my life locked into a hostile intimacy with America's wrongness. Conditioned and brainwashed to hate myself, and my own race, other black people became my prey and the Crips my sword. Though I cannot condone it, much of the violence I inflicted on my gang rivals and other blacks was an unconscious display of my frustration with poverty, racism, police brutality, and other systematic injustices [. . .]

Here, we digress to note the fact that Tookie's radical change in consciousness ultimately sealed his fate. To be brief, as reputed co-founder of a notorious street gang, he stood before the eyes of the state as a potential "messiah" with influence enough to "unity and electrify urban guerrillas across AmeriKKKa to take a stance—in the spirit of Alprentice Carter — against state sponsored terrorism. On that note, it is imperative that we recognize the fact that these guerrillas are to the State what Christian Parenti aptly characterized as "social dynamite":

> Social dynamite is that segment of the population which threatens to explode; the impoverished low-wage working class and unemployed youth who have fallen below the statistical radar, but whose spirits are not broken and whose expectation for a decent life and social inclusion are dangerously -alive and well. They are the class that suffers from "relative deprivation." Their poverty is made all the more unjust because it is experienced in contrast to the spectacle of opulence and the myths of social mobility and opportunity [. . .].
>
> It is a threat to the class and racial hierarchies upon which the private enterprise system depends. This group cannot simply be swept aside. Controlling them requires both a defensive policy of containment and an aggressive policy of direct attack and active destabilization. They are contained and crushed, confined to the ghetto, demoralized and pilloried in warehouse public schools, demonized by a lurid media, sent to prison, and at times dispatched by lethal injection or police bullets. This is the class--or more accurately the caste, because they are increasingly people of color--

which must be constantly undermined, divided, intimidated, attacked, discredited, and ultimately kept in check with what Fanon called the "language of naked force." (Parenti, 1999)

By the mid-1980s, the snake had again shed its skin. Ronald Reagan, still begrudged with the fact that the Black Panthers had marched onto Sacramento with firearms drawn, left the governor's seat in California to settle the score by using the presidential powers of the United States to effectively stamp out the remaining remnants of political dissent amongst AmeriKKKa's poor. Shortly after arriving in Washington, President Reagan would declare a pretentious "War on Drugs" after CIA backed guerrillas (i.e., the Contras) had dumped tons of cocaine and high-power assault weapons into urban AmeriKKKa. The effect would be forthright. As if it happened overnight, we went from mentors of humble origins and kids breakdancing on the block for fun, to knocks (i.e.) drug addicts) and domestic terrorists without conscious, armed to the teeth eager to rob, steal and kill for the spoils of the crack-trade. "Dope-Boy-Magic" instantly made millionaires of some of the most deprived and marginalized elements of AmeriKKKan society who became gods of a newfound religion: material gain over life!

    The value we once placed on community solidarity was transfixed to a "BLOCK" claimed by a gang which, inadvertently, caused our communities to become a "place" not to be respected insofar as the greater community was concerned, but rather a place to make war and Dope-Boy-Magic. Thus, a generation and culture sprang up of corrupted morals, disrupted families, and ultimately, a dismantled "Village" no longer capable of cultivating a progressive youth as comparable to previous generations. Reagan had effectively created his own prey. For the machinations and propaganda surrounding the War on Drugs would, in effect, cast upon us an image of menacingly evil, and thus the ghetto came to symbolize a bivouac from which urban predators terrorized the city. This in turn exacerbated both public fear and the call for the hunt and capture of young Afrikan and Latino males.

    Again, to be brief with this history is unkind. Yet the various forms of terrorism that came of this can be summed up with the following phrases: "Racially Disparaging Drug Sentencing Laws," "Mandatory Minimums," "Massive Prison Construction Boom," "Mass Incarceration," "Prison Industrial Complex," "Militarized Police Force," "Single Parented Homes," "Record Political & Voter Disenfranchisement," "Antiterrorism and Effective Death Penalty Act," and a number of other acts and phenomenon which were what Parenti described as, "defensive policies of containment, aggressive policies of direct attack, and active destabilization of young Afrikan and Latino males."

    By the turn of the century, statistics would report the damning consequences of these policies. The United States, with just five percent of the world's population, had succeeded in ranking number one with the highest incarceration rate per capita. Some 2.3. million people were in prison or jail, with another five million on some form of supervised release. Of which, one (1) out of nine (9) black men (ages 20-34) were locked up and our sisters were joining them at three times the rate compared to white women. Notably, some

5,000 people per year are killed behind bars due to prison and jail officials refusing to provide adequate health care (Smith, 2015). Even more, a glaring sixty percent of all reported arrest-related deaths from 2003 to 2009 were found to be homicides committed by law enforcement, which totaled 2,931 people killed by the police (Gardner, 2016). For those of us who are fortunate enough to survive our prison experience, we often return to economically devastated communities where statistics report every 28 hours a black man, woman, or child is murdered by the police (MxGM, 2012).

At this point, we believe it safe to say Black Lives Matter did not develop in a vacuum in and of itself. Rather, it arose from a peoples' continuous and courageous struggle to combat the anti-humanity evils of white supremacy that have evolved as the snake continued to shed its skin again and again throughout history so as to maintain the "philosophy" through a racist system of laws, policies and institutions that seemingly have regressed to its former self with the blatant demands that we submit to white authority or die by police bullets. That said, if history has been any indicator of all that is or can become of Black Lives Matter, then we must be careful in not allowing ourselves to be duped with arguments of police reform. For people have rallied and protested for police reform since the very first police forces were created some 200 years ago. And by little measure has there been a significant change in the fundamental relationship of the police in service of the state. Therefore, we conclude by making the following point: police terrorism is not a problem that can be fixed by a mere change in policy. For it is a symptom of a far greater problem that is rooted in an unjust system built on a philosophy" that ultimately must be done away with. Otherwise, we stand to make the mistake of previous generations that were pacified with the snake merely shedding its skin only to remain a snake by nature to strike again at some juncture in the future as history repeats itself.

I Want to Live

Not Enemy Combatant
Abdur Nadheerūl-Islam

White people, mostly republicans, conservative, with right-wing Christian propensities, spew racist blatant stupidity that "tries" to confuse and deceive the peoples of the world about whether or not Black lives matter, with moronic statements, "all lives matter" or "blue lives matter," two arms of the same monster. This of course is to whitewash or cover up the historical and present social rejection and social destruction of American Black peoples. The white settler nation has always been animated by its hatred for black people. It is apparent American white society has always created white unity by expressing Black disunity, or white lives by Black death, or white equality with Black inequality. This is a white American structural arrangement which continues from chattel slavery. A brutal exploitative system of Black psychological and physical death that obviously persists today.

Consider since just 1980-2017 Black homicide rates have been roughly 10,000-gun deaths from a 20,000 to 38,000 overall murder statistic. That means, in 37 years there were approximately 370,000 Black murders—mostly by Black-on-Black violence, gun deaths (of course this is a probable estimate). The American politicians know this. The American educators know this. The American business leaders know this. And the murderous, warmongering police forces of America know this emphatically. Yet, the so-called Sunday political pundits promote a desensitized representation of genocidal racist destruction of Black peoples. This deliberate social murderous state-of-affairs must come to an abrupt end. Unequivocally and completely.

The Black Lives Matter organization and movement must transform and become an institution for a new Black Reconstruction and re-socialization of not only Black communities and movements by every movement that joins in active solidarity against the white supremacist state. Not just a political protest exercise. That means that wherever Black American people reside in numbers, Black Lives Matter must achieve political and economic power and independence. People who have been subjected to chattel slavery, domestic and international colonialism, Jim Crow De jure and De facto segregation — which plays into mass incarceration, pre-school to prison pipeline, strategic police state genocidal murder, Black-on-Black murder and violence, gentrification and high unemployment, abject poverty, disease, malnutrition, infant mortality, and low life expectancy, etc., should have their first objective as political, economic and social independency and power (self-rule), rather than white supremacist political jargon like integration. Self-determination, self-direction and self-definition, not assimilation, acculturation, or subjects to cultural imperialism. Adopting the social, cultural and political ideology of any form of a "white supremacist" doctrine or "indoctrination." That is our Black collective condition. The forced indoctrination then the conscious acceptance and even promotion of white supremacist ideals and/or ideology. Conservatism — capitalist political control ideals to maintain monopoly — racist capitalist and imperialist power, wealth and influence or indoctrination: the psychological control over man's mind and behavior (the thought leadership).

The conscious deceivers, consistently deceive, and we-the-people grow up in a false environment, institutionalized, and we all become false peoples of a false consciousness. Promoted to keep all of us — the people — confused, conflicted, disputing, fighting, killing, and dying: poor and powerless. Just how the capitalist powers want it. We must acquire political power to create the institutions that will inevitably create a stable, wholesome, and "free society." Not just demanders, but decision makers and legitimate creators of a new functioning reality for peaceful, clean, stable, well fed, well worked, and loving and caring communities. A true human society of wellbeing and safety. Free healthcare, free education (all levels), free childcare, and financial family benefits. A socialist principle and ethic: creating state/city owned corporations or manufacturers that pay a "real wage" and will pay for the "free" social governmental services, generating wealth or revenue for renovating public works, new highways, bridges, roads and buildings – that which can withstand super-storms of destructive forces or global Katrina.

Black Lives Matter must create worker cooperatives, where the workers own the corporation and/or manufacturers and share profits and pay scales. Substantially raising the wealth gap between black and whites: equally. Black peoples (and all people really) need to adopt a social doctrine that teaches the principles and values of our true human nature. Uprightness, goodness, love, kindness, gentleness, kindness, self-restraint, self-control, self-discipline, self-preservation (that which promotes Black social unity), equality, compassion, reason, generosity, human connectivity, celebration of our separate and distinct cultures and ethnicity. The philanthropic — the holistic — love of humanity and all of the social benefits of a loving and unified community and nation. Culture that makes all our people conscious, knowledgeable, perceptive and principled; uniting the people and suppressing anger, hate, insult, abuse, sexual indiscretions, fighting graphic violence, abuse, harm, and misogyny.

Making people strong, thoughtful, and responsible is the key to ending gun violence. And having a stable inclusive, diverse and fair system allows people to satisfy their financial needs and establishes a community that is wealthy, prosperous, and productive. A community of social respect, social unity, social peace and wellbeing. But this cannot occur if the Black Lives Matter activists just be activists. They must become reality makers, and real, true brokers of power. The police cannot murder Black men and people if police are in the control of smart, strong, and worthy political leaders' people that do not all U.S. citizens to be considered "public enemy" and gunned down like war enemies. They are U.S. citizens — not "enemy combatants." Until we can secure complete political power, a citizen review board with military-style disciplinary and "imprisonment' powers over the police, must be established to control police brutality and police murders.

I Want to Live

United States citizens must not be gunned down like dogs, pigs and mules! They are dignified human beings. It is not a conspiracy theory! It is a stratagem! A strategy is a plan and pattern. The plan is pure violence against Black people and it is a pattern because it happens all across the country. This is a genocidal strategy to initiate a violent confrontation with the Black community and U.S. Citizens. We must not allow this! We must, I repeat — secure political and economic power. To head off national armed conflict.

Be a reality maker! Re-define our world! Black lives do matter. When Black lives seize the means of power, they will matter. Save You.

Black Biography as Analysis of Society
Kevin Curley

As a kid growing up in South Central LA, I had to endure a poverty-stricken upbringing. The kid in me back then couldn't place a face on hate, and fears which were created only came from witnessing the Los Angeles police department harassing Blacks and Hispanics, never really traveling outside the inner city. I grew to believing white people wouldn't accept me because of the targeting by white police officers. I participated in the 1992 LA riots, and a child experiencing a threat and an all-out press by the national guards, after the smoke cleared, led me to believe authority figures such as cops carried a serious evil for Black people. Growing up in the ghetto of south LA witnessing white police officers killing minorities, I never felt they were roaming the urban areas to protect and serve all. All I ever knew what to do whenever a cop car drove down my street was to run and hide, praying not to be shot in the back.

I was a juvenile, tried as an adult at the age of 17. There was no valid evidence to convicting me other than hearsay by people in my neighborhood who were coerced felons, to place me at the scene of a crime of murder. I was found guilty by claimed peers of my community, but the panel of jurors never set foot in my neighborhood and favored a skin complexion which was not of a recollection in the surrounding area in which I grew up in. In the 90s, when I was at last free and living in the free world, children I grew up with were never properly informed through the educational system; or recreational centers. The stigmas that'll be placed on a young kid by being Black, witnessing attacks and murders on black people by cops, was the reason I felt neighboring schools never educated urbanites on Black history.

Growing into life through the California Department of corrections, having become self-educated and awakened by studies, made me aware of a truth about hate. I've managed to gather an insight that Blacks were enslaved and sold, kidnapped and traded to folks, because on certain lands, slave masters wished to use black people for their self-benefits. Black people were not brought to America or other countries to succeed, but for personal gains by the oppressors. The strength carried out by the rebellious overthrew the evils. The creation of African Americans fighting for equality drove an uprising to protect Blacks throughout the world, and the activists led a united force giving Black people the same rights as white people.

In the millennial era, black people still are not given the same equality as white people as a converted Jew by choice. The Black culture can't relate to the atrocities Jewish people endured. Being able to relate to the pain, I honestly can say there's still a whole lot of work to be done on the driven energy naysayers create. Pegging minorities being the problem, what makes it so bad to convict cops and racial radicals still trying to annihilate a people? Society can't blame murder by cops on Black people, and society shouldn't defend a corrupt judicial system. Videos and media broadcast televised programs don't lie. When the world views murder committed on black people by cops, there's never really no need to draw out the question if Black lives matter, because the obvious can easily be answered when all facts have been proven. Black people must continue fighting for their voices to be heard. Hate comes from jealousy and the lack of emulating a unique being. All creative aspects which have become an artistic talent from Black people and by black people, it draws an envy from the less-gifted and less talented.

Why Should We?
Kevin Curley

The matter (the flesh and blood) of all Black life matters. I sit with my thoughts and emotions as a juvenile tried as an adult in a California state prison. I reflect on my life daily, wishing I knew then what I know now at the age of 39: reality, when the obvious effects serving a sentence of 35 years to life is played out. Having to endure a harsh and cruel conviction, many can lose hope and lose many dreams. As a Black man converting to Judaism, I relate to the cruelties Jews and Africans had to endure during times before my existence. I can admit Black lives matter, not just from the strength the people carry, but also with our will to forgive. Walking in the here and the now, being created in the image of G-d, I send out my prayers to all evil-doers and ignorant mankind who judges

G-d's creations by the color of their skins and poverty-stricken lines, carrying a universal education as my daily research and studies to influence myself and others to create a voice, believing that all humans are created equal, place me in a mindset of peace. Even though I live and deal with hate from many, being created with a darker skin complexion, I know I matter and all which look like this Black/Jew and all those that look like me. Strangely, I have to be more protective of myself and many actions, but being socially conscious rewards me on my drive to lead by example, living through the messages and fights of those before me begging for equality.

As a Jewish Blackman, I know the stigmas placed upon me by the ignorant forces my voice to be even louder, yelling peace and unity for all. I can't judge media-broadcast televised statements and individuals in positions of politics, displays of verbalizing hate and their will to wanting the minority buried underneath them, because politicians didn't give the minority people a voice. Susan B's, Dr. King, Malcolm, Fredric D., among other Gods, woke up the world to their dreams. I personally learned from mentioned educators that, in order to count, you must be accountable for your own actions. Black lives matter when black people make them count. To uplift the people, you should never allow yourself to being bought. Why accept payment, when the 40 acres were never promised? I smile for the visionaries and I breathe in their strength; because without freedom fighters and major sacrifices, black people may not have ever existed, have never become a Toby, or sing for Rosa P. Neither one of them gave up their seats. So, why should we?

*This essay has been originally published as a zine by True Leap Press.

I Want to Live

Ain't I a "Prisoner," Too?
Stephen Wilson

In a recent article, Dan Berger wrote, "Prison reform is now in vogue." It's so true. Right now, everyone, even Kim Kardashian, is proffering solutions to the carceral quagmire we've sunken into. Intensified public scrutiny of policing and hyper-incarceration has led to an increase in the discourse about "crime," policing, and imprisonment. Many Americans agree with The New York Times editorial that stated: "The American experiment in mass incarceration has been a moral, legal, social and economic disaster." People are beginning to understand that prisons and policing are repressive tools of the state, which are critical to the maintenance of power. But in this interval of seeming possibility, some prisoners have good reason to feel anxious.

The American Prison Movement is made up of a wide range of people and organizations with diverse goals, but one consistent trait still runs throughout the entire movement: privileging the straight, able-bodied, cisgender male viewpoint. When the experiences of prisoners are represented, they are typically the experiences of cisgender men, usually Black or Brown, who are straight, able-bodied and neuro-typical. However, there is no monolithic prisoner experience. Our experiences with policing and imprisonment are far from universal; they have always been inflected by race, class, gender, sexuality, ability, and geography. How will this one normative definition of prisoner free us all?

When prisoner is posited as cis-het, able-bodied men, the lived experiences of the most vulnerable prisoners—queer, trans and disabled folk—are at best marginalized, or at worst delegitimized and erased. We need to consider how policing and imprisonment affect particular populations. Poor, Black transwomen are not targeted, policed, and locked up in the same ways that Black/Brown cis-het men are. "Seeking to understand the specific arrangements that cause certain communities to face particular types of violence at the hands of the police and in detention can allow us to develop solidarity around shared and different experiences with these forces and build effective resistance that gets to the roots of these problems." (Morgan Bassichis, Alex Lee, and Dean Spade, *Building an Abolitionist Trans and Queer Movement with Everything We've Got*.) By making the multifaceted ways the PIC affects us all visible, we are able to create a wider base of support. But we are stymied in our efforts because our definition of prisoner continues to exclude the most vulnerable incarcerated folk.

There have been interventions in the continued marginalization of the most vulnerable populations. Organizations like Black & Pink and the Sylvia Rivera Law Project vigorously advocate for and amplify the voices of queer/trans prisoners. Texts like *Eric Stanley and Nat Smith's Captive Genders: Trans Embodiment and the Prison Industrial Complex*, Kay Whitlock, Joey Mogul, and Andrea J. Ritchie's *Queer (In)Justice: The Criminalization of LGBT People in the United States* and Ritchie's *Invisible No More: Police Violence Against Black Women and Women of Color* center queer/trans lives in discourses on policing and prisons. But in national conversations about policing and prisons, queer/trans prisoners are largely overlooked. We continue to live in the white spaces of books and articles on what to do about mass incarceration and policing. Our views remain absent in the debates. And what goes unheard may be of the utmost importance.

In *Captive Genders*, one reads: "gender, ability and sexuality as written through race, class and nationality must figure into any and all accounts of incarceration, even when they seem to be nonexistent." Yet many people in the American Prison Movement refuse to consider how the intersections of race, class, gender, sexuality and ability affect encounters with police and imprisonment. In *Queer (In)Justice*, the following is stated: "By bringing queer experiences to the center, we gain a more complete understanding of the ways in which race, national origin, class, gender, ability and immigration status drive constructions of crime, safety and justice." There is no way to bring conscious and liberatory politics to the work of our movement without focusing on all the main pillars driving the PIC, including homophobia and transphobia. It is only by centering the lives of the most vulnerable that we can ensure that no one is left behind. We have to start asking ourselves serious questions. What becomes visible when we listen to the experiences of the most marginalized people behind bars? How could that listening strengthen our movement?

Many activists, inside and outside, are reluctant to ask: what is gained from emphasizing queer/trans encounters with police and prisons? They don't question why queer/trans prisoners' issues tend to run parallel to, instead of intersecting with, other prisoners' issues. Queer/trans prisoners feel unsure that our concerns will be addressed by other activists. We wonder if our pain is taken seriously. And this should not be the case. At every stage and moment of the American Prison Movement, queer/trans folk have been present and involved. We have struggled and suffered alongside, and often because of, straight, able-bodied, cisgender males. Our issues remain unheard. We have not been silent; we haven't been listened to. Even during the most rebellious years, prisoner uprisings linked their conditions with critiques of American capitalism, racism and imperialism, but not homophobia or sexism. We have no seat at the table. And just as former US Congressman Barney Franks said: "If you're not at the table, you're on the menu."

The reason queer/trans prisoners have no seat at the table is because many activists, especially incarcerated ones, don't consider us part of the struggle, the movement. Those who do rarely get beyond performative solidarity: statements of support and concern. They won't struggle alongside us. Our tradition of anti-police/confinement work is often ignored. The antagonism between queer/trans folk and the state predate the current incarceration boom. "Because prisons, police, immigration officials, and psychiatric institutions have long punished people for transgressing sexual and gender norms, queer and trans people have a long tradition of resistance to institutions of punishment" (S. Lamble in Captive Genders). Might there be something to learn from this tradition? The self-oriented only perspective of many activists precludes them from seeing the value in queer/trans traditions of resistance and the importance, rather the necessity, of struggling alongside us for survival and liberation. It makes me wonder how they define community?

There are unspoken closures of community that many need to reflect upon. Who is included in our definition of community? Who is excluded by intent or omission? Queer/trans prisoners are not struggling in the prison movement simply to add a different viewpoint. We are challenging the fundamental definitions of freedom, safety, justice, and community. Moreover, we are challenging the very definition of prisoner and calling for the recognition of all prisoner experiences in this moment of possibility. We say loud and clear: You will not live upon our ruins. It is time for other prisoners to know that "All of us live in a culture that is attempting to limit the range of our humanity, and so we're all in this liberation struggle" (Rebecca Solnit). The laced-up minds of some activists prevent them from understanding that "constructive criticism and self-criticism are extremely important for any revolutionary organization. Without them, people tend to drown in their mistakes, and not learn from them" (Assata Shakur). The need for self-criticism and the role we may be playing in oppressing and silencing others cannot be overstated. "The true focus of revolutionary change is not merely the oppressive situations which we seek to escape, but that piece of the oppressor which is planted deep within each of us" (Audre Lorde). We are against all the systems of oppression that prop up the prison industrial complex, but are we working to uproot the oppressor in our hearts—white supremacy, homophobia, transphobia, sexism, ableism, xenophobia? Are we able to acknowledge differences without devaluing them? Moreover, can we recognize differences among prisoners and use these differences to expand our visions of justice, freedom, safety, and community? This is the challenge.

People are becoming more aware of the race and class-inflected aspects of policing and incarceration. We have to do more to educate them about the gender and sexuality-inflected aspects. And we need to do it as a movement. As everyone offers their solution to mass incarceration and police violence, let us remember that failing to recognize and affirm the intersections of race, class, gender, and sexuality erases the lived experiences of many people behind the walls. Let us remember that "reform without a vision of fundamental change, without a politics that aims to leave no one behind, can give way to new forms of captivity and containment by the state" (*The Long Term*, see introduction).

The Eyes of a Revolutionary Made in Prison
Lonnie B. English Bey

Through the eyes of an imprisoned revolutionary, it's hard to see and truly understand the struggle and resistance being caged behind bars of steel and cement because of the so many limitations being placed on you; of what you can have and what you can't have. Then you have to fight the administration about things that you can have by mail; rejecting the item or items. When you're being upright, independent, and fearless and standing up for my divine principles of love, truth, peace, freedom and justice against racist pig guards working to oppress all prisoners in the State of Michigan Industrial Complex or MDOC, and not to mention prisoner or prisoner oppression which goes on throughout the prison system. It's hard to be a revolutionary in prison when standing up for justice, equality, and human rights causes a lot of stress, pain, and sometimes disappointment, when trying to get out of prison on parole and getting turned down because of your steadfastness for the cause of truth, justice, and righteousness of the struggle.

Sometimes finding yourself in the hole, not for something that you did, but because your name was mentioned, or helping stop a guard pig from brutalizing another prisoner, or helping another prisoner file a complaint for violating a prisoner's civil rights. Sometimes standing in solidarity with other prisoners for something that's rightly needed and necessary, but finding out that you are the only one in the hole or in level V for the cause. It's hard as hell being a true revolutionary behind the walls with very little or no support from the outside world and standing your ground for what's right. Through the eyes of an imprisoned revolutionary fighting to stay out of the bullshit that's going on around the yard on a day-to-day basis; trying to stay focused on the real issues, eating chicken of different kinds four times a week, potatoes 365 days a year, and a lot of turkey the other three days a week. And doing more time than any other state in the country: 120%. That's 100% of your minimum sentence, an extra 60 to 90 days or 6 months over your minimum sentence. In 2018, in this state, there are at least ten-thousand prisoners past their minimum sentence who are still incarcerated. Also, in this state, they have a law called, "Truth-in-Sentencing" that was passed in 1998 or 1999, in which every prisoner has to do 100% of their time with no "good time" whatsoever. There are a lot of young men who don't have any kind of education — ignorant in many ways — but think they know it all, yet don't know, not at all, especially regarding their rights, civil or human. In the state of Michigan, we don't have a real strong advocate for prisoners, or a prisoner movement either, but that's going to change in the future — we truly hope.

The Prisoners Movement itself is not that strong because as long as they can go to the prisoner store and spend $126.00 a month, get JP5 plays and songs, get TV's, visits, telephone calls and order items like gym shoes, etc., they are satisfied with their living conditions of being treated worse than animals; dogs and cats, and they don't stand up for themselves at all. Through the eyes of an imprisoned revolutionary, all I know is the fight, struggle, and resistance of the powers that be from oppression, exploitation, imperialism, and racism, etc., always thinking and working for the good of humanity — striving to bring justice and truth to those who really want or need it. Thinking in tactics of changing things for the betterment of all people in the world. I truly understand oppression and its source which came from people who have power and control over the resources that all people need and use in their everyday lives, like political, economic, and social control over society; the rich European elites. These are the real enemies of revolutionaries because we are fighting, struggling to overthrow their ideology of the so-called white supremacist, and their fascists friends' ideas and views.

The rich control society and the businesses, and the poor have to work for low wages to survive off what they earn and they will do better but without the means. As revolutionaries, we want to take the riches from the rich and give it to the community, and let these communities manage and govern these resources to even the playing field; bring some equality to the poor. This should be done not only in the U.S., but all over the world, especially in third world countries. Through the eyes of an imprisoned revolutionary, this unjust society with its institutions must be abolished because this whole country's foundations were based on racism and so-called white supremacy from its political, social, economic and culture; was evil from its beginning.

Now, looking at its court system, or corrupt Department of Justice, where for the New Afrikan or Afrikan, there is no true justice when it comes to our justice. Look at reparations. Everyone has them, but not New Afrikans. I don't have to name the people who have received them, but not the New Afrikans who are descendants of Afrikan slaves. Yes, New Afrikans live in the poorest communities throughout North America. I think the U.S. government has been playing tricks about this citizenship on the Afrikan people and this is why they have been abused, misused, beaten, attacked and molested by Europeans all these years without any reap from justice. There is a case that was decided by the U.S. Supreme Court that has never been overturned from 1853-1857: the Dred Scott vs. Sanford case where the court ruled in part, "That all Afrikans that were imported into the U.S. to be slaves, they shall not be citizens of the U.S.; nor free born or any of their descendants, or if they are emancipated shall not be citizens according to the U.S. Constitution."

The Preservation of Slave Psychology
Wayland "X" Coleman

The Thirteenth Amendment of the United States Constitution permits slavery to be used in our prisons. Because of that, the prison industrial complex has become a safety deposit box for the preservation of an old draconian mentality that promotes abuse and dominance over others. The interesting thing about our society today, is that most of our society doesn't believe that slavery still exists in Amerikkka, and would be vocal against a public display of it — at least in most states, I hope. despite the way society feels about slavery today, the slave ships, plantations, and the niggers are alive and functioning.

Sometimes the simple changing of the name of something can make people look at it differently, and even in an accepting way. For example, have you ever heard of Cream C? It's a treatment for really bad acne, or eczema. One of the two, but that's not the point. Cream C is an ointment prescribed by the dermatologist and given over the counter. The trick is that Cream C is just plain old Crisco. So, in reality, people who use Cream C are just rubbing Crisco on their breakouts (but it's the best treatment for it, so don't be unpersuaded). People would think differently if you told them, "just rub some Crisco on it." The point here is that slavery by another name is still slavery, so let's look at the change of the labels.

Slave ships were used to transport captured Africans. The Africans were bound by chains with cuffs and shackles, and stored in cells. They were brought to the plantations where they would go through a physical and psychological breaking. The label "Human," "Man," or "African," was stripped away, and the new label, "Nigger," was forced to be accepted. The label "Nigger," created a sub-species that society would accept as no more important than a dog or a work ox. In this way the "person," could be treated in any manner, even killed, without any consequences. Now let's compare.

Paddy wagons transport captured citizens. The citizens are bound in chains with cuffs and shackles, and stored in cells. They are brought to the prisons where they will go through a physical and psychological breaking. The label "Citizen," "Human," or "Person," is stripped away, and the label "Inmate," is forced to be accepted. The label "Inmate," creates a sub-class — or species, for the sake of continuing with my terms — that society sees as no more important than a dog's needs, or the trash that they take out. In this way, the "Person," could be treated in any manner, even killed, without consequences.

As we can see from above, the terms have simply been switched. Today, prisons are the plantations. They have sweatshops where prisoners — which is the new label for "slave," — work to earn a measly forty cents per hour, with hopes that they will be promoted to the ultimate dollar fifty per hour. So, prison = plantation, prisoner = slave, and inmate = nigger.

Sometime in early 2000, I read the literature of William Lynch, titled, "Let's Make A Slave Kit." After studying his proposed "breaking" methods, I realized that his methods of breaking an African into a Nigger, was still being implemented in breaking a citizen into an inmate. The elements of establishing psychological fear and dominance are consistent. The only difference is in the tools. The beating mechanism was a whip. Here, it's a riot shield and mace. In Willie Lynch's work, he emphasized the importance of breaking the will to resist, by making cruel public examples out of those who were brave. Though he laid out many brutal methods of making an example out of the rebel, his most famous method was the method of tarring and feathering. In his method, you took the biggest, worst African, dumped tar all over him, doused him with feathers, tie his arms and legs to two horses pointed in opposite directions, light him on fire, and whip the horses while everyone watched the horses pull him apart. This brutality was used to instill the fear of God into the onlookers, so that they would be afraid to resist. Prisons still use the tar and feather approach in many ways to keep its "inmates" submissive. This comes in the form of sanctions, solitary confinement, and beatings.

I do not consider myself to be a slave. I do recognize the current implementation of old slave breaking methods, and I recognize the importance of labeling. I do my best to use the term "incarcerated person" in my dialogs, however there are occasions where I will use the term "prisoner;" i.e., I am a prisoner rights activist. I think the term "inmate" dehumanizes us in the same way that "nigger" was designed to dehumanize the Africans. I also expect that my use of terms in this writing can be offensive to some of the readers, however, the same way that one feels about the old language should be how they feel about the new. The intent of the labels is the same. "Inmate," should be as offensive to you as "Nigger." Because you are not offended, those old slave teachings remain well preserved in the prison industrial complex.

UNITED STATES CONSTITUTION

Amendment XIII

Section 1:

Neither slavery nor involuntary servitude, except as a punishment for crime whereof the party shall have been duly convicted, shall exist within the United States, or any place subject to their jurisdiction.

Cowboy Boy Up
Donnie Phillips

Once upon a time, here in this wild, wild, western hemisphere, there resided a brave type of integrity; a strict decorum of courage which we now know as "The Cowboy Code." A certain type of bravado which would come to define a very important strand of American culture: 1. Never shoot an unarmed man (or woman). 2. Never shoot a man (or woman) in the back (whether armed or unarmed) — period!

There was never no need for sheriff body cameras or lengthy investigations because there was nobody sinister enough to try to qualify or justify such an act. You were very simply (and roundly I might add) deemed a coward and then hung. Now had some Mayor Giuliani emerged back then proclaiming that his cowardice was suddenly reasonable due to the danger, the caution for guns and the cowboy's proclivity for violence, someone might have cut him off and yelled, "Get a rope!" However, as a wise OG I empathize, I recognize his gang mentality of blind loyalty to a deeply rooted group dynamic. I know he and many boys in blue feel unfairly targeted. I can remember in South Central L.A. in the mid-80's when the real boys in blue, the gangs were roundly castigated for the drive-by shootings as innocent women and children kept getting hit so we had to listen, even despite our concerns and heightened risks of being shot we renounce our own practices and elected to 'cowboy up.'

I'm a grandfather of three grandsons. I'm mildly educated and extremely matured so my values have changed considerably in these last 25 years so I don't air t pile on and scream that "Black Lives Matter," although of course they do. I merely wish to add a bit of context and advice to these back-and-forth exchanges. Each person an officer kills out there is an individual living and surviving with the same fears that cops claim they are dutifully enduring, except we, the people experience it twenty-four hours, seven days a week while the officers merely collect a check, get training, body armor and a gun all in the name of fulfilling an eight-hour shift so it can't be too much to ask, no…to demand, that these officers stop it with their fears and to "Cowboy Up."

I Want to Live

No Justice, No Peace
Raymond Springs II

My opinion on and about Black Lives Matter as a member, or citizen of the Nation of Gods and Earths held as prisoner of California's injustice System is this: that for far too long women, Black women, Brown women and other non-white women have continued to be marginalized in western world countries (white societies) in the credit they have received in the past and now in our present day on the lines of movement leadership. This can often apply to many white women also, due to their oppression by the Global White Supremacy System's total ideology of white male dominance, chauvinism and continual repression of all women. Many of them were leaders in the Abolitionist Party who fought to free the slaves, hid slaves who escaped plantations on the Underground Railroad system, also in the suffrage movement. Even now many of these white women use their privilege to assist Black and Brown, Yellow and Red Humans the world over and have a position to play in the larger movement with the goal of complete Freedom, Justice and Equality for All people.

However, this is about the women's Leadership of Black Lives Matter that began as a hashtag post on the net by Alicia Garza, a beautiful Black and Latin woman who lived in Chicago after the sanctioned police murder of 18year old Michael Brown, of Ferguson Missouri. A movement that grew and mobilized black and brown bodies to do peaceful marches, take political action, build a network in many cities and locations across the mainland United States with Chapters in Puerto Rico, Hawaii and Guam. These chapters are led by women like Michelle Abdullah, a professor at UCLA who is conscious about how this system of "Global White Supremacy" which is a term I've borrowed from Dr. Frances Cress Wesling's, "The Isis Papers," (which is a must read) is waging wars again black bodies through lethal force used by this nation's law enforcement agents, or policy men/policemen. For these women who founded this movement, there's been attacks on their sexually, up surges in arrest on their person's, and women of non-white origin and much propagandism by the media (media is a weaponized branch of global white supremacies mind control over working class populations the world over) the latest messaging came in the form of comparing the late Dr. King's non-violent approach to civil rights with the continual struggle of Black Lives Matter, this is the visionary history created in actual time while black men are still being murdered by these policy men/policemen who is none other than members of the United States urban insurgency and surveillance program with their overt actions and secret agendas to annihilate non-white bodies housed in these ghetto and project areas.

Our protection is the cell phone images and the almighty voices of our Queen Mother's, Black Lives Matter. Michelle Alexander in The New Jim Crow, provides the continuation of the attack against the non-white population in these United States since its inception, to right now, with statistics and the Apologist Narrative. You know we are sorry for flooding non-white areas with heroine during Vietnam, cocaine during the Contra wars in South American and now with heroine from Afghanistan, and the creation of Crime Culture born out of its effect, yet we don't feel responsible enough to suspend the prison policies and sentences we imposed during this period of time. (Read Dark Alliance by Gary Webb and know that the C.I.A. brought drug lord to the U.S. and connected them with poor non-whites, and in many cases sold and distributed rock cocaine themselves. This book is a must read) these apologists are fraudulent and lip Service to an oppressed people. The fact that Black Lives Matter is dealing with the age-old problem of racism, and the murder of black bodies in these United States is an indication that the peaceful civil disobedience philosophy of yesterday, along with integration into white society does not solve the problems. We non-white are continuing to have problems created and acted on by agents of the Global White Supremacy System.

In today's world, through the economic slavery of low wages and the cost of living, most our people can't afford to march, get involved in the civic problems, nor afford righteous defenses when faced with the courts and (in)justice system. This is the same as the 1900's during the Black Codes and Convict leasing under Jim Crow rule because they could pay the thirty-dollar fines. Now bail is too expensive and lawyers too expensive so deals are forced on the innocent, and if and when a citizen fights the case with a public defender (an officer of the courts) the prosecutor has an endless budget to get a conviction while the defense has a very small and limited defense and are also the defense of hundreds of citizens a week, making it impossible to spend enough time on each case to launch a proper defense.

The Black Lives Matter has created the environment and political climate where hashtag Me Too, hash tag Times Up are fighting the global white supremacy systems for equal pay for equal work while Megan Marco was made to leave her job as a successful actress in order to marry Prince Harry, furthering this chauvinistic culture of inequality and male dominance. This women's Movement has waged war against "Sexual Harassment and Sexual Violence," both of these are a part of Western Culture from its conception where cavemen oppressed their women and assigned them powerless roles in society in religion, politics, workers class home lives and even sexual objects. Sadly, many of these accusations are the result of new found social power and not truth, being that these accusations destroy a man's life in the court of public opinions. I believe Black Lives Matter will be the vanguards of the truth finding the women who lay fraudulent claims are guilty of the worst crimes, the crimes found in the wrong usage of power. Women being the first teachers will help the world's population toward the humanization of all people. Helping males see their superiority in field of negotiation unknown to them in thought and action. These Women of Black Lives Matter are the queen Auset, Candice, Nzinga and countless other goddess embodiments of the great feminine energies and intelligences that create balance in our world; past, present and future.

An equilibrium unexperienced during any period of western civilization, with special attention paid to our time in a false modem era where women bodies and sex are objectified at a continuously rising rate with the excuse of morality. A huge example being sex workers; an industry made almost entirely of women, receives a negative stigma, reputation repudiation and even criminalization. One due to the exploiter class of this industry being mainly made of men, with characters from Hugh Hefner to Iceburg Slim, a street pimp, now human trafficking. All these are painted with the brush of immoral acts or oppression which implies force. No one is engaged in the task of understanding how and why women using logic and freedom of choice enter all levels of this industry as a means to live the lifestyle that this affords them. Even women in this society are brainwashed into believing no intelligent woman would dare exchange sexual acts for currency, even when the history of this industry is so well known. Black Lives Matter as a vanguard party should fight for these women's rights to use their bodies in any way they want legally, without all the negative insults, criminalization and dangers associated, they should be respected. No matter their chosen professions. Period.

Black Lives Matter needs a prisoner outreach program due to one in three African American males, at least once in their life, end up in jails, prisons, on probation, parole, or some legal form of supervision. Though they make up only 8% of the entire U.S. population, many of these prisoners need a true education about women; women of a non-white origin, especially women's positions in this society, and women's positions in all the African American movements in the U.S. and the Western World in general. These prisoners need relationship classes in order to break the European stereotypes taught to them by everything from a formal education to media, including cartoons and music, role assignments, and finally, how to work collectively with women in the movement world, and be an ally to them — a protector, respecter, and lover of our Sisters on every level with respect of creating a more correct culture and social dynamic on each level of reality.

Reality-based education from the world's first teacher; the Asiatic Black Women. Non - white women, who through western hiring practices was, and is, removed from the home, where original children of all cultures grow up feeling inferior. Paying and hiring practices that are mostly equal to that of the women, white women, while paying and hiring black men far less, creating a role of gender strife, and inter-radial disunity. It does not matter that the majority of the leadership identify as lesbian, Black Lives Matter can help both genders (biological) learn what it takes to forge a successful relationship based on needs and responsibility complimentary assignment. These where well known by the Nation of Islam's F.O.I and M.G.T members and expounded on from ancient time as described in great detail in Metu Neter's *The Destruction of Black Civilization*, *Message to the Blackman in America*, and other historical books that came from times that predate the western world's revisionist history. The 3-fold meaning gained by the initiates taught the esoteric meaning of mythical stories and parables, which shows and proves the truth of women's leadership and Maat Laws institution as beneficial to all peoples. This is a future door that can be actualized by the Black Lives Matter movement, once funded and organized along with Times Up. The life of members born into the black dysphoria the world over needs to except Women as the Embodiment of Auset (Isis) and a Maat, the rightful leaders of the Asiatic Black Dysphoria and the whole world's only chance to united peace, respect for nature and natural laws, scientific discoveries that lead to cures to diseases instead of just money driven treatments. These women of Black Lives Matter and Times Up are the embodiment of the ancient Goddess class known to the Golden Priest Case of Khamit.

One thing that I must point out in this essay is socialism as a goal to end the continuous destruction of Black lives that is a direct effect of capitalism, which has its birth in the transatlantic slave trade, where black bodies became property, this is the major reason the United Sates is one of the most powerful and advanced nations in the world today. That the law enforcement agency was born as slave patrols, that the American psyche thrives on racialization. As a member of the united struggle from within, I urge Black Lives Matter to join with all organizations fighting for reparations and capital redistribution is very country state or territory who got rich through Afro-asiatic exploitation past and present. Find out about the venerable Queen Mother Moore, The Republic of New Africa, James Forman book, The Making of Black Revolutionaries, NBPC, N'COBRA, African Reparation Movement (ARM), The Conyer Bill (originally HR40, now HR91), to start with. Yet, with GoFundMe, there should be an ongoing campaign to collect one dollar a day from Black Mother's supporters to self-solve poverty issues by creating millionaires every day out of older working and/or retired mothers so that 1) they can finish paying off their home, bills, and retire. 2) so that they can level wealth to be inherited by their children. That would change many peoples of color beginning years. Affording them advantages that have only been experienced by whites and Asiatic people with culture still intact.

WARNING: "Today, during the post-civil rights era, most black feel that the goals of the sixties have not been fully achieved. Here, hindsight suggests that the end of the sixties represented the waning of the cycle, a civil rights cycle." "A "cycle" is described as a "course or series of events or operations that recurs regularly and usually leads back to the starting point" …. But in this regard, it is easy to forget the beginning and the end of the first civil rights cycle, roughly 1868 to 1896, the period in which civil rights issues related to the constitutional ratification of the thirteenth, fourteenth, and fifteenth amendments were bitterly contended in a struggle in which black civil rights advocates were beaten down in abysmal defeat. It would be almost sixty years before the American racial climate would sanction the enactment of another civil rights cycle" (Cruse, 1987, pp. 7-8). Now we are about another 60 years in our future of today from the future and fight for civil and human rights by icon giants the likes of Malcolm X, martin Luther King II, Ella Baker, Rosa Parks and so many more leaders in yet another "cycle." Black Lives Matter, please learn the many lessons from our past struggles in order to break the "cycle" and to finally advance.

I Want to Live

Just an Introspective Look
Brandon Dixon

America, did you know that you can invest in the prison system on the stock market, or shall I say invest in prisoners? Because without Prisoners there are no Prisons. Which is why if they build them, they will fill them (Prisons). This is represented by the fact that in the 90's, President Bill Clinton accomplished a record 10 billion prison building boom (Sentencing and Justice Reform Advocacy (SJRA) October 2011 Vol. 3, Issue 7). The annual collection of prisoners' nets billions for zealous investors. Former Vice President, Dick Cheney, was one of the biggest investors in the prison system. Well, when there is nearly 2. 2 million individuals incarcerated on any given day (SJRA April May 2014 Vol. 6, Issue 1), (a ratio of 500 people per population of 100,000) at an estimated incarceration cost to the government between $32,000 to $57,000 annually (as of June 2003), I would be investing also. That's a lot of money to be had. I'm not mad at the way investors invest their capital, that's capitalism at its best. But what does have a thorn in my butt is the way that the government obtains the people they put in prisons.

In spite of the current recession, prisons are one of the most successful businesses in the American economy; more so than most colleges/schools. Speaking of such, did you know that the prison system is better funded than the education system? Well, it's true. The government disregards the fact that it costs substantially more to house and maintain a prisoner for 12 years, than it would cost to feed, house, clothe, mentor, and send a child to school from grades K-12 — or to send young adults through college. For example, California built only one college since 1980 versus 21 prisons, and invested about $9.6 billion in prisons versus $5.7 billion in the whole University of California system. They also spend approximately $8,667 per college student versus $45,006 per inmate (Hindsight is 20/ 20 by Donnie Phillips 9-2-13/ Time Magazine 2-2-2012). Investing and encouragement in school has become somewhat taboo in the inner city. However, since people of color have created creating ways out of the hood for themselves and others and have demonstrated a profound ability in acting, directing, writing, and producing their own movies and music, the government took notice and slashed, or completely done away with funds intended for music and media classes in the ghettos.

An example of this can be seen in Mr. Andrew Cuomo's campaign for the Governor of New York, which he based on the morals and principles of "Robin Hood," to 'take from the wealthy and give it to the needy.' Mr. Cuomo won on this premise. As the Governor of New York, he cut about $1. 3 billion from schools in 2011. This caused thousands to be laid off, and cuts were made to pre-school, advanced placement, career and technology courses, sports, arts and music programs. Governor Andrew Cuomo did the very opposite of what he claimed he would do in his campaigns. He literally cut twice as many funds from the poor school districts than he did from the wealthy school districts. Politicians like Governor Andrew Cuomo exist throughout the nation — they say that they're for the people at voting time; once elected they often hurt the very people that they claim to be for.

These things in turn make it difficult for young people to want to go to school, as well as have the incentive to go to school. It's my personal opinion that such cuts and elimination of educational programs leave young people in the inner cities with a lot of free time on their hands to speculate and give in to temptations of sex. The designed lack of interest in school, could be a direct/indirect cause of the high rate of teen births high school dropouts. Groups with the highest rates of teen births, ages 15 to 19, are Hispanic girls at 83% births per 1, 000, and Black American girls at 68% births per 1, 000. In the year 2000, high school dropouts of men, ages 20 - 40 years old, were 32. 4% for Blacks, 6. 7% for Whites, and 6. 0% for Latinos. The majority of the inner-city teenage moms and/or high school dropouts find themselves seeking governmental subsidies, succumbing to criminal and gang activity, falling into drug use and/or find themselves dwelling in the streets — making themselves easy prey to law and order.

With a prisoner yielding upwards of $32, 000 annually, if I were a part of the establishment, I would have the (foot soldiers) navigating the muddy waters of the ghetto's ridden with high school dropouts too — harvesting its people like crops. The only ones that care are the very people in that community. But they are too focused on struggling to survive, plus they feel their voices aren't loud enough to be heard. I'm not saying that the government is all bad, but the establishment creates these communities (ghettos), offering a prime opportunity to have their foot soldiers (police) do and say whatever it takes to force arrests, manipulate cases, and enforce convictions. Novella Coleman, Staff Attorney with the ACLU of Northern California, stated the following in the "Sentencing and Justice Reform Advocacy" journal:

> Because of racial profiling, people of color are more likely to be targeted for arrest and prosecution. The severe underfunding of the public defender's office, which serves many people of color, is just another manifestation of the racial bias inherent at every stage of our criminal justice system — from the moment of arrest, to charging decisions, to bail determinations, to selection of jury members, and to verdicts and sentencing. While people of color make up roughly 57% Fresno County's population, they represent over 69% of all arrests in the county.
>
> —"Sentencing and Justice Reform Advocacy", *SJFA*, Vol. 7., Issue 3, June-July 2015.

Michelle Alexander titled her book, *The New Jim Crow: Mass Incarceration in the Age of Colorblindness*. This is what's going on to fatten their pockets - like I said it's Capitalism at its best. This reflects the 2008 arrest rate in California which was 49% per 1, 000 for black girls, 8. 9% per 1, 000 for White girls, and 14. 9% per 1,000 for Latinas. Moreover, in the year 2000, men aged 20-40 were jailed or imprisoned at rates of 11. 5% for Blacks, 4. 6 % for Latinos, and 1. 6% for Whites.

Now I ask, are Blacks really doing more crime than other ethnic groups? I doubt it, but it's obvious to me that the government's primary targets are the poor working class, disenfranchised urban tribes, financially stricken masses, and those least thought about; Skid row inhabitants, which are predominantly found and harvested from ghettos. This high-tech genocide and modern-day lynching are all in the name of profit(s). In America, the invisible population (prisoners) are nothing more than three-fifths of a human being. According to the U. S. and the California Constitutions, prisoners are nothing more than slaves — literally! It's true that the neo-Slavism existence of prisons, are one of the most profitable, effective, tyrannical, complex components in the government's arsenal. Prison, by its very nature, enforces its anti-social, anti-family, anti-community, anti-rehabilitation, anti-self-respect, anti-dignity, anti-parole, anti-self-worth, anti-self-identity, anti-Islamic, anti-education, anti-life, anti-culture, and anti-freedom, but promotes self-contempt, self-hatred, and self-loathing upon its population. The inmate has begun to embrace the establishment's tyrannical ways- they're even down-playing the known neglect; the psychological effects, and the social destruction, that it is causing prisoners, and their families and friends to undergo.

Nonetheless as we (prisoners) try desperately to maintain mind, body, and spirit under the repressive hours, days, months, and years spent isolated, exiled, and separated from family and friends. Prisoners are denied basic freedoms, suffering in these new plantations that are stretched across the nation. Prisons are occupying prime agricultural land; enforcing its inhabitants to manufacture and package goods, such as, but not limited to: cookies, milk, bread, T - shirts, socks, shoes, chairs, tables, eyeglasses, etc. (See: www. catalog. PIA. CA. GOV). I ask you (America) why is the government taxing you to house inmates (e. g "In California Taxpayers fork out an astounding $14 Billion a year to operate "CDCR"), (*SJRA* Vol. 7, issue 4, Aug.-Sep. 2015), when the prison system possess the facilities that can manufacture enough items to be purchased by consumers in order to clothe, feed and pay its employees (inmates) minimum wage? These prisoners can then give back as a way of restorative justice, as well as sustain itself to warehouse these human beings.

Epilogue

about . . . Inner Child Press International

The U.S.-based Inner Child Press was founded in May, 2011 by William S. Peters, Sr. as a subsidiary of Inner Child Enterprises. The founder already had an extensive experience when his writings and publications are concerned. Mr. Peters' first book went into print without his awareness in 1972. In 2008, he self-published a collection of his own poems, My Inner Garden. Inner Child Press grew out of his desire to self-publish his own literary work, which subsequently led to assisting other writers in the publishing process.

From its early years on, Mr. Peters' writer-oriented vision and his staff of established writers have been embraced by novice authors as well as those who had been previously published. Inner Child Press has diligently preserved its original mission – writers for writers – as it grew into a globally distinguished publishing company, starting in September, 2011. A poetry contest resulted in the first edition of World Healing World Peace (published in April 2012). The call for submission was open to poets from all over the world. This anthology was a significant first step for the company to enter the paradigm of international recognition.

As time progressed and Inner Child Press began to publish more authors across the globe – individually and in anthologies, its international presence expanded. This growth also led to Mr. Peters and other board members making appearances at international poetry festivals, to include Kosovo, Macedonia, Lebanon, Morocco, Tunisia, Jordan, Palestine, and Canada. They also made multiple appearances across the United States. The founder's visionary tutelage, along with the company's dedicated board members, thus enabled Inner Child Press a formidable international image which led to Inner Child Press International.

Inner Child Press International, ICPI, is an integral instrument to empower the voices of writers from all regions of the world through literature and strives to leave an essential footnote in the history of humanity. William S. Peters, Sr. and everyone at Inner Child Press International envision that literature, especially poetry, possesses a unique ability to bring people together. ICPI is very adamant with its stance and has therefore appointed cultural ambassadors from every region of our world. This all-inclusive approach epitomizes the company's motto, 'building bridges of cultural understanding'.

Thank you.

Inner Child Press International

'building bridges of cultural understanding'

www.innerchildpress.com

Inner Child Press International

'building bridges of cultural understanding'

Meet the Board of Directors

William S. Peters, Sr.
Chair Person
Founder
Inner Child Enterprises
Inner Child Press

Hülya N Yılmaz
Director
Editing Services
Co-Chair Person

Fahredin B. Shehu
Director
Cultural Affairs

Elizabeth E. Castillo
Director
Recording Secretary

De'Andre Hawthorne
Director
Performance Poetry

Gail Weston Shazor
Director
Anthologies

Kimberly Burnham
Director
Cultural Ambassador
Pacific Northwest
USA

Ashok K. Bhargava
Director
WIN Awards

Deborah Smart
Director
Publicity
Marketing

www.innerchildpress.com

Other
Socially Important Anthologies
By

Inner Child Press International

Inner Child Press Anthologies

Advisory Board
World Healing, World Peace Foundation
human beings for humanity

worldhealingworldpeacefoundation.org

Inner Child Press Anthologies

Inner Child Press International
&
The Year of the Poet
present

Poetry
the best of 2020

Poets of the World

Now Available at
www.innerchildpress.com

Inner Child Press Anthologies

Inner Child Press International

presents

W.A.R.

We Are Revolution

Poets for Humanity

Now Available at
www.innerchildpress.com

Inner Child Press Anthologies

World Healing World Peace 2020

Poets for Humanity

Now Available at
www.innerchildpress.com

Inner Child Press Anthologies

the Heart of a Poet

words for a better tomorrow

The Conscious Poets

Now Available
www.innerchildpress.com

Inner Child Press Anthologies

Now Available
www.innerchildpress.com

Inner Child Press Anthologies

Now Available at
www.innerchildpress.com

Inner Child Press Anthologies

Now Available at
www.innerchildpress.com

Inner Child Press Anthologies

Now Available at
www.innerchildpress.com

Inner Child Press Anthologies

Now Available at
www.innerchildpress.com

Inner Child Press Anthologies

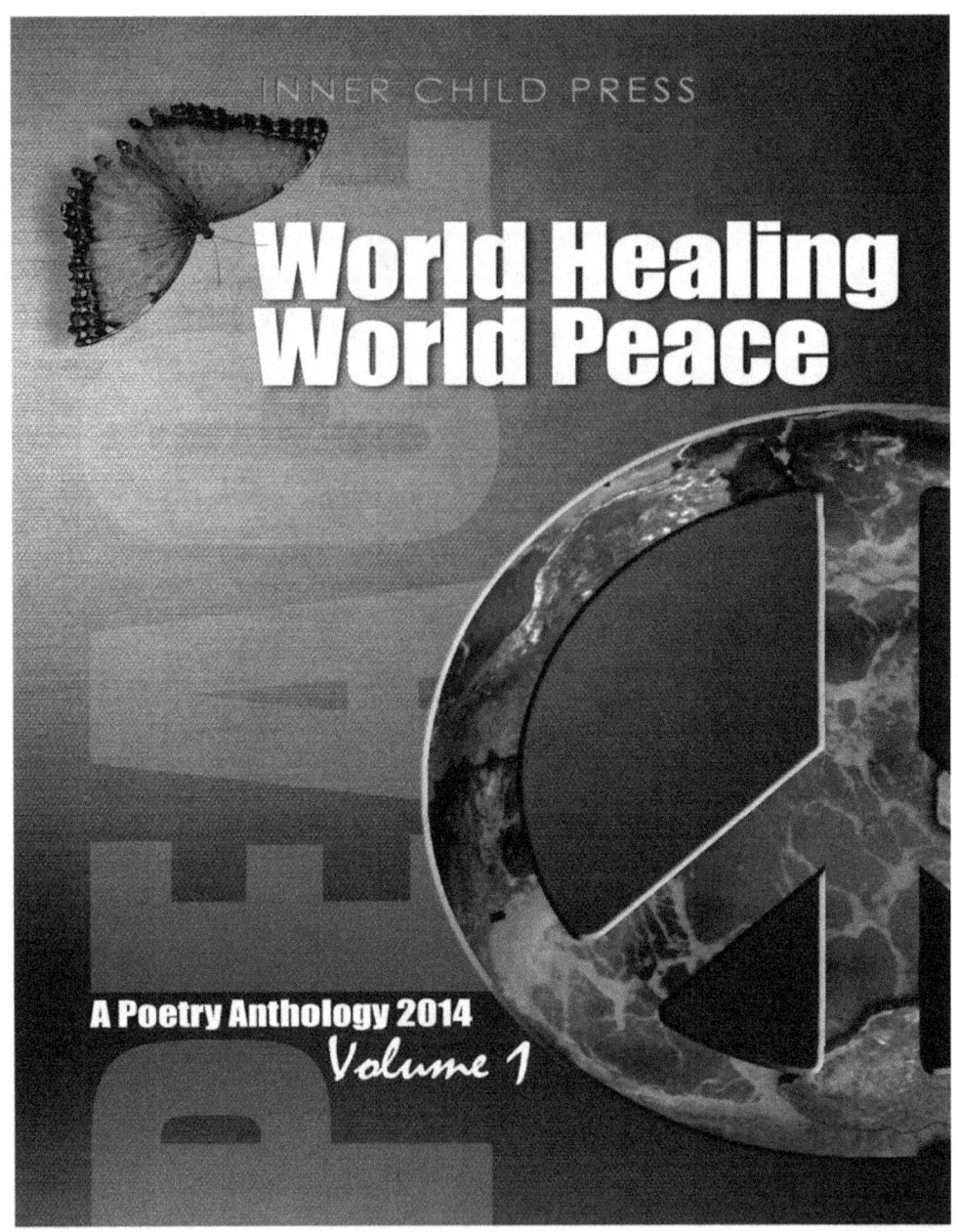

Now Available at
www.innerchildpress.com

Inner Child Press Anthologies

Now Available at
www.innerchildpress.com

Inner Child Press Anthologies

Now Available at
www.innerchildpress.com

Inner Child Press Anthologies

Now Available at
www.innerchildpress.com

Inner Child Press Anthologies

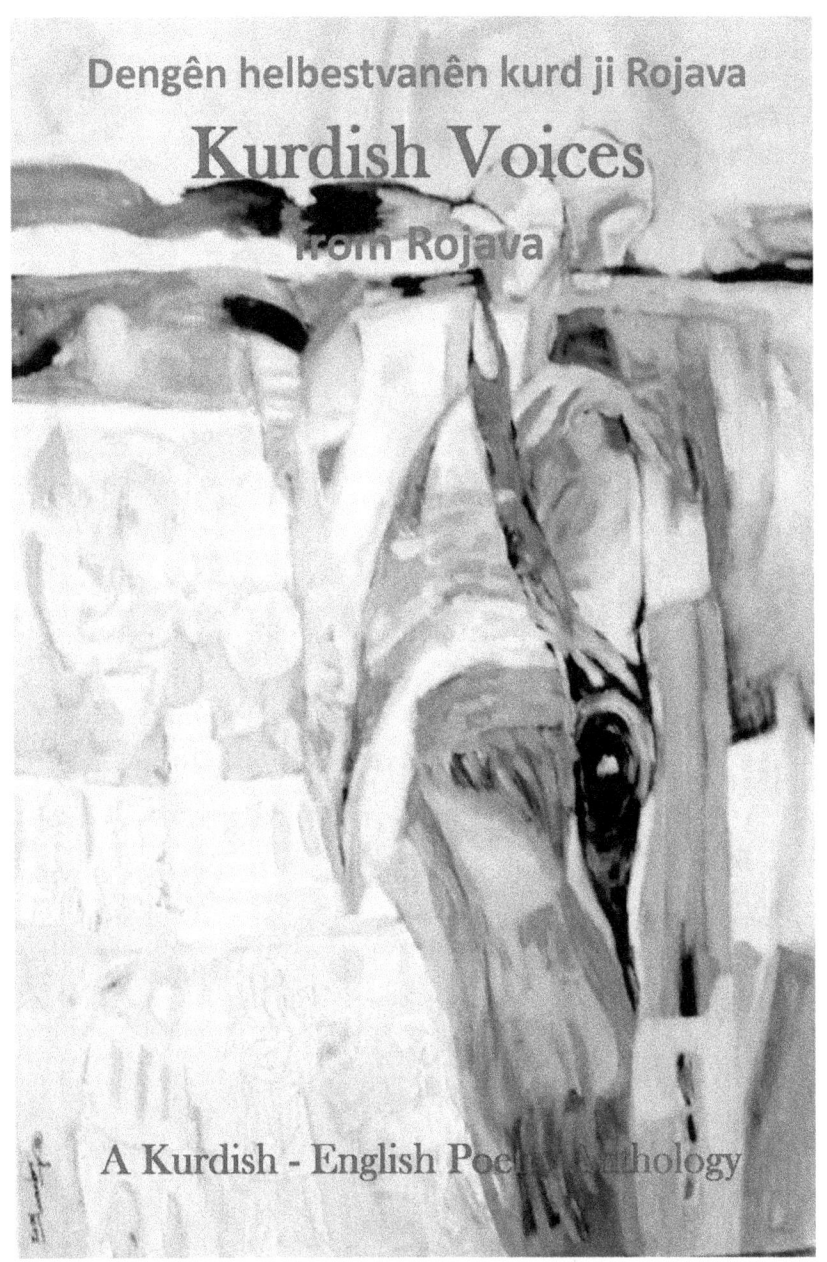

Dengên helbestvanên kurd ji Rojava
Kurdish Voices
from Rojava

A Kurdish - English Poetry Anthology

Now Available at
www.innerchildpress.com

Inner Child Press Anthologies

Now Available at
www.innerchildpress.com

Inner Child Press Anthologies

Mandela

The Man

His Life

Its Meaning

Our Words

Poetry . . . Commentary & Stories
The Anthological Writers

Now Available at
www.innerchildpress.com

A GATHERING OF WORDS

POETRY FOR
TRAYVON MARTIN

Now Available at
www.innerchildpress.com

Inner Child Press Anthologies

Now Available at
www.innerchildpress.com

Inner Child Press Anthologies

Now Available at
www.innerchildpress.com

and there is much, much more !

visit . . .

www.innerchildpress.com/anthologies-sales-special.php

Also check out our Authors and all the wonderful Books Available at :

www.innerchildpress.com/authors-pages

www.worldhealingworldpeacepoetry.com

Inner Child Press International

Inner Child Press International is a publishing company founded and operated by writers. Our personal publishing experiences provide us an intimate understanding of the sometimes-daunting challenges writers, new and seasoned, may face in the business of publishing and marketing their creative "Written Work".

For more Information:

Inner Child Press International

www.innerchildpress.com

intouch@innerchildpress.com

'building bridges of cultural understanding'

www.innerchildpress.com

www.ingramcontent.com/pod-product-compliance
Lightning Source LLC
Chambersburg PA
CBHW080502110426
42742CB00017B/2971